INTERSUBJECTIVITY AND CONTEMPORARY SOCIAL THEORY

For Liz and Katharine

Intersubjectivity and Contemporary Social Theory

The everyday as critique

HOWARD FEATHER
City University and University of North London

Ashgate

Aldershot • Brookfield USA • Singapore • Sydney

Published by
Ashgate Publishing Ltd
Gower House
Croft Road
Aldershot
Hants GU11 3HR
England

Ashgate Publishing Company
Old Post Road
Brookfield
Vermont 05036
USA

Ashgate website: http://www.ashgate.com

British Library Cataloguing in Publication Data
Feather, Howard
    Intersubjectivity and contemporary social theory : the
    everyday as critique. - (Avebury series in philosophy)
    1.Social sciences - Philosophy 2.Popular culture -
    Philosophy
    I.Title
    300.1

Library of Congress Catalog Card Number: 99-76641

ISBN 1 85972 281 4

Printed in Great Britain by
Antony Rowe Ltd, Chippenham, Wiltshire

Contents

Preface and Acknowledgements

The essays which make up this volume took shape over a period of around five years, during which some took the form of papers and others emerged out of teaching programmes. The whole work spanned periods of working at the Open University, Middlesex University, the Universities of East and North London, and City University.

I am indebted to colleagues there, past and present, and to members of the Radical Philosophy Collective, who, of course, bear no responsibility for the outcome. Thanks are due to Ted Benton, the late Brian Darling, Jean Grimshaw, Stuart Hall, Barnor Hesse, Annie Nixson, Peter Osborne and Nirmal Puwar for discussion points or comments on parts of the manuscript, and I am particularly grateful to Kevin Magill for his detailed comments on two chapters.

An immeasurable debt is owed to Liz and Katharine, without whose endless forbearance and support this book would not have been possible and to whom it is dedicated.

Thanks also to John Spelman of Avalon Associates for his much valued assistance with the presentation of the final copy of the manuscript and his attempts to keep the writing on schedule.

(References to Dummett's *The Interpretation of Frege's Philosophy* are sometimes given by the abbreviation 'Frege-Dummett').

Howard Feather
1999

Introduction

This collection of essays is envisaged as a response to two sets of interlinked debates. Firstly, there are the issues around the role of ideology in cultural analysis, that is, whether a certain kind of Marxist analysis, the Frankfurt School critique of popular culture, is adequate to the task of grasping the complex formations which comprise popular culture and of evaluating their content. Secondly, there are the questions posed by discourse theorists against Marxists and others about the role of language and cultural classification systems, and their relation to formal institutional discourses and practices.

In all of these debates the nature of agency, or more concretely, subjectivity, is of paramount importance. The role and the *wider* significance of subjectivity, its *world* character, or the 'objectness' of the subject (Adorno, 1973, p.164-5, 174ff), its claims to embody an objective reason, needed to be reassessed. This had to be done in the light both of a reductionist, 'base-superstructure' perspective operating from within Marxism and a pessimist determinism from Foucauldians and others, which had close affinities to fatalist readings of Weber's rationalisation thesis.

How could a response promoting the objectness of the subject be formulated in the context of cultural analysis? The notion of *sense* in Dummett's reading of Frege's theory of meaning offered a way forward. This suggests that our ideas about knowledge and truth emerge in only a roundabout way and cannot be read off literally from cultural artefacts and activities; that is, seen as reflections of economic priorities or conventional and dominant definitions of those things, as the Frankfurt School tended to argue.[1] On the other hand, there was a 'prejudice' that classification systems predetermine what kinds of things we can talk about or construct subjectivity through discursive positions in some direct way.[2] Hence views about culture tended to oscillate between these two overlapping positions.

Dummett proposes an idea which offers a way of circumnavigating these positions to give subjectivity a world dimension. This is encapsulated in Frege's claim that sense determines reference. That is, classification processes emerge from discursive practices via a trope of grasping the sense of subjects' utterances from the meaning context in which they are embedded. In this view 'sense' provides the link between an active reflexive subjectivity and the wider environment which structures its activity. Dummett's point is that effective communication or structured discourse starts from a practised context of shared meanings and only on that ontological basis can classification take place, that is, make sense to subjects. Hence classification is an outcome of communicative practices rather than its starting point.

It would follow from this that the discursive power of circulated statements depends not on classification itself but the capacity to share amongst others the senses embedded in cultural practices, to draw them, *intersubjectively*, towards a discursive project. This means that the precise nature of cultural configurations starts not from conventional designations but from situated practices through which reference to significant cultural objects is the outcome, and this involves negotiation or contestation of the conventional meanings. Classification is then always contested (dialogical) and problematic. To suggest otherwise, that is, that classification determines the sense we have of things results, as Russell famously demonstrated, in a paradox. Crudely and simply, this is that to name or refer in this way entails that the name pre-exists what it classifies, but, on the other hand, it must already have the name in order to be recognised as a thing of that particular sort!

This prejudice about how classification works throws up ambiguities of the sort that when we describe something as 'biological', say, then 'biological' seems to serve both as a name and also as the thing named. For Frege, unease about this would be a consequence of a faulty view about what referencing objects means; his response to this unease would be that the name and object are not really separate at all, that conceptual objects are always situated by some predication and that we fall into this predicament because, for instance, we are mislead by the syntax of language into dividing the world into subjects and predicates. Rather, objects are precipitated from the contexts of linguistic interaction, whose structure they resemble in their own; classification systems bear the mark of the contexts in which they arise, expressing the complex articulations of sedimented meaning found there. They are situated rather than conventionalised/universal structures.

The book is structured as a series of interlinked essays through which the central concepts intersubjectivity, sense and the everyday, are examined with a view to exploring the critical and utopian potential of a phenomenological perspective. This is done mainly via a dialogue between various strands of phenomenology and currents within Marxism and postmodernism.

Notes

[1]   See Kraniauskas (1998) for a current example of this, that is, the discounting of a rationality situated in the everyday of popular cultural forms.

[2]   McNay (1994, pp.76-7, 82) examines the absence of real subjects in Foucault's formulations of discourse and suggests the need for analysis of informal, everyday structures, to understand the scope of formal institutional arrangements.

1 Making Sense of Social Subjects: Reflexivity, Perception, Praxis and the Everyday

The various threads of argumentation in the following chapters can perhaps be best outlined through a fairly brief overview of key issues which illustrate the directions of enquiry and their relation to aspects of phenomenological social theory.

The recent discussions over several volumes in the Culture, Media and Identities series of meaning, representation and discursive practice provide a convenient focus and point of departure for outlining and bringing together central themes in the field of communication.[1]

Making Sense

Probably the most important question, the question within which other topics are framed, concerns the way meaning is produced or constructed socially and it is in the first of the series of publications referred to (du Gay *et al.*, 1997) that the process of communication, of 'making sense' is introduced. This is done via a case study, the development of the Sony Walkman.

Specifically, the problem faced by the supporters of some new idea, as represented here by the Walkman, is how to explain or communicate its meaning to the public (*ibid.*, pp.13-14). An early description identified the invention as a 'smallish stereo-headphone cassette player'. This raises two facets of communication. Firstly, the description means something because it taps into existing meanings such as 'stereo', 'headphone' and 'cassette player'. Thus it offers a whole genealogy, a historical narrative involving listening to radios and record players via headphones, stereophonic records, tape recorders, cassette players and so on. Secondly, and more importantly perhaps, the description of the Walkman is not a literal account but uses the kind of background narrative mentioned to give the artefact a meaning. The Walkman, hence, is not literally a smallish stereo-headphone cassette player, but as the authors indicate, the expression operates as a metaphor which enables us to grasp what is going on.

The conventional meanings of the terms involved here are situated within wider semantic networks, fields of connotation which convey a precise though non-literal meaning or sense of the object depending on the practical purposes in which a conversation about the Walkman is embedded. Specific discourses, those of 'Japanese-ness', high tech, youth, mobility, for example, may be connoted. As the writers observe, 'we constantly draw on these wider connotations and discourses to make sense of an object, to expand or specify its meaning' (*ibid.*, p.15).

Now the idea of the metaphorical character of everyday language, the indexicality of natural language utterances, where meaning rests largely on context which provides the images through which meaning is communicated, is well known. The metaphor via its situational imagery condenses a variety of meanings and enables conversants to 'get the point'. In its everydayness it runs together the old with the new, the familiar and the strange as is seen in the genealogical basis of making sense of the Walkman (the object is like a small stereo-headphone cassette-player).

The homogenising of an object with its background features (it's like this) is a key aspect of its everyday reception. The authors emphasise that to understand something it must become 'part of our cultural universe' and paradoxically in order to belong it must also be seen as different. Further,

> [this] means that the Sony has become inscribed in our informal social knowledge - the 'what everybody knows' about the world - without consciously knowing where or when they first learned it. This kind of shared, taken-for-granted knowledge is an essential element in what we call 'culture'...Belonging to a culture provides us with access to such shared frameworks or 'maps' of meaning which we use to place and understand things...The Walkman is now firmly located on those 'maps of meaning' which make up our cultural 'know-how' (*ibid.*, pp.9-10).

Reflexivity

The everyday mode of making sense by plugging into semantic networks is a kind of mirroring which enables us to pick out or give meaning to an item such as the Walkman. The account of this given in Moores (1997) stems from Giddens (1991) who argues that reflexivity is a kind of self-monitoring, that is, self-examination, through which we can adapt our behaviour to situational requirements. Giddens' (Moores, 1997) view of reflexivity as a kind of learning and response process has us picking things out and then feeding them back into the field of activity concerned. If we take the example of the Walkman, this would mean identifying certain semantic networks in which the Walkman is found and then relating these to other networks through which we can use the machine. For instance, one could use it whilst skating, rollerblading or travelling on the 'tube'. The machine alludes to other modes of reception via its headphones, cassette and radio elements, but then this in turn is tied into our personal appropriation of it as rollerblader, etc. Similarly, a musician could pick up on an idea in the discourses of say, rock music and feed it back into their next album by making allusions to the background, founding influences on their own style. Hence it is often argued à la Giddens that there is in contemporary life a growing self-conscious relatedness to historical and cultural background.

In a sense this seems right, that is, background ideas help to pick out Walkman features or a musical style. However, there is a difficulty in that the musician's project, for example, is in this way seen as something separate, that is, something which is come by separately, from the background, which, it has been argued, helps to pick it out and identify it. On the Giddens view it is as if the musician has ideas about a project first and then identifies some historical contextual allusions with which to embellish it. This seems to put the cart before the horse as it is the context which enables the project to emerge in the first place. The project is able to identify itself only by reference to its background features. It is this self-referential nature which delivers the project to us as a possibility, that is, it is feasible because it already connects with our existing, taken for granted semantic networks.

In Dummett's (1981, p.132) world of common linguistic practices, this entails that we are already doing or enacting the project, before we can name it. That is, the monitoring is incorporated in the project before we come to recognise that we are doing it. Following this line of thought, it is appropriate to note Merleau-Ponty's position that we construct the rationality of what we are doing rather than referring to 'rationality ...given beforehand', 'we make sense out of our experience from within it' rather than from outside it. Thus meanings are received from experience rather than given to it. This 'being-in-the-world' (following Heidegger) is then the monitoring process, 'the activity of organizing the world by responding to it from within...' (Merleau-Ponty, 1971, x-xi).

The contextual is therefore already embedded in subjectivity and it is then via 'unconscious' or 'informal social knowledge' that the conscious self grasps an object. The reader will have noted some tensions in the readings of reflexivity in the Culture, Media and Identities series but also the proximity of phenomenological sociology and structuralist ideas in positing identification as a process involving oppositions, and in a 'dethroning' and relegating of the conscious subject to the role of a reader/communicator already positioned by semantic networks it inhabits.

Intersubjectivity

Whilst Thrift (1997, p.197) refers briefly to the work of Heidegger, Merleau-Ponty and others as establishing variants of a locale of shared meanings (the place in which we dwell, and so on) as embodiment or lived experience, it is worth turning to Merleau-Ponty for an elaborated account.[2]

As mentioned above, the subjectivity or identity of the Walkman user is already permeated by the context in which it moves. Merleau-Ponty (1992, pp.238-9) makes a similar point about subjectivity which he sees as both constituting and constituted by its object, which is never totally distinct from it. There is, in our parlance, always an element of self-referentiality in attempts to distance ourselves from, objectify features of the world. Indeed, if 'I break with the critical attitude, I live the unity of the subject and the intersensory unity of the thing, and do not conceive them after the fashion of analytical reflection and science'.

The bodily character of the subject's perceptions ensures that they are always situated perceptions rather than those of a detached observer or 'God's eye view'. Hence the subject is not, *pace* Hegel radically distinct from what it observes, 'a hole in being', but rather 'a hollow, a fold, which has been made and which can be unmade' (*ibid.*, p.215). Hence we do not wholly control the field of perception which 'we' observe around ourselves. Rather we are immersed in it and it always has a generality which escapes conscious organisation. As a sentient being experiencing the world, we embody a mode of existence which runs through us without our being its author (*ibid.*, p.216). Kruks notes (1990, p.119) that this is not an embodiment of the collective as in Heidegger's *das Man* (the 'they') but rather takes in the trajectory of the self and its projects and the way they have become sedimented in its experience. As such, she cites Merleau-Ponty, the perceiving subject 'is not myself as an autonomous subject, but myself in so far as I have a body and am able to "look"' (Merleau-Ponty, *op. cit.*, p.240). Kruks concludes: 'if such a self is not a Sartrean for-itself, nether is it a 'constituted' self, or an 'effect', as for example Foucault or Lacan would argue' (*loc. cit.*).

Rather, Merleau-Ponty argues that in its relation to the other (other subjectivities) the embodied or intersubjective subject can overlap with other subjectivities which are mutually situated in some way and it can also attempt to exclude or negate these subjectivities. Both modes are essential to the embodied subject.

It is important to note here that for Merleau-Ponty conflict arising between individuals is not to be interpreted within a paradigm of dyadic interpersonal relations (the 'micro-level') as is so often the case in the work of phenomenologically-oriented sociologists. Rather, the key frame of reference for the intersubjective subject is *institution*. Individuals are suffused in the situational particularities associated with different projects or interests. There is an autonomous dynamic at work here which links individuals into the general and conflictual relations taking place at the level of politics and 'public' history.

Conflict itself is not reducible to the institutional arena of class struggle but pervades our always institutionally mediated encounters. On the other hand, individuals are born into different positions with different commitments and projects. Hence '...the ambiguous mediation of social institutions and play of contingency are irreducible aspects of politics and of history' (Kruks, *op. cit.*, p.139).

For Merleau-Ponty, intersubjectivity is not founded as it is with the Habermasians on primordial consensus or reciprocity of interpersonal relations, but rather it contains a negativity due to the tendency towards pure subjectivity which characterises the individual subject's self-consciousness, as in Hegel's account of the desire for self-recognition. For example, our self-understanding may occur through ideologies of individualism which become part of the shared language of self-recognition. But for Merleau-Ponty this is always institutionally mediated and this introduces not only negativity as discussed above but also contingency. The conflictual nature of social projects, situations and intersubjectivity results in their contingent quality. We thereby conclude as authors of things we never consciously intended, although we may have some *sense* (intimation) of the direction of events (see below). Merleau-

Ponty sees this 'discordant intersubjectivity' not only in class struggle but also as a general feature of social relations.

The situatedness of experience therefore lends itself to negativity or contradictoriness within the intersubjective and hence gives a contingent quality to historical events. A tradition, a project or line of thought which makes sense can suddenly become *non-sens* (Kruks, *op. cit.*, p.139). A useful way of illustrating this point might be to think about fashions in things, and to take the word 'fashion' as generic, emblematic of contingency in social life. In economics, the Keynesian, welfarist conception displaces pre-war monetarism and is in turn displaced by Thatcherite monetarism. In technology, clockwork gives way to electrical power, but then clockwork-powered radios and laptop computers appear. In science and its ideologies Darwinism displaces catastrophism, is briefly displaced by sociological perspectives on evolution and now (1990s) neo-Darwinian explanations are found for almost everything. Art Deco styling achieved a new lease of life in the 1980s, as did the (1930s) filofax, and so on. None of this is meant to suggest that social life is inherently whimsical, rather that the way its semantic networks come together to frame new objects is, in any detail, unpredictable. The Walkman again serves to illustrate the point: the narratives of radio, walkie-talkie, the cassette player, etc. fuse in an innovative way which, incidentally, highlights the global nature of meaning structures, as du Gay *et al.* (1997, pp.42-48) note.

If we understand all this as situation, as the interaction of profoundly disparate biographies and situational trajectories, then we can grasp the unevenness of intersubjectivity. Under such conditions, although situations configure individual biographies it is difficult to extricate the two. An individual's decision to leave or enter a situation looks contingent but at the same time it is suffused in the generality of social life and hence the experience of situatedness, Merleau-Ponty argues (Kruks, *op. cit.*, p.143), exceeds any conscious awareness of it. Therefore, within the dual aspects of intersubjectivity, any encounter can be looked at either from the viewpoint of individual decisions which precipitate it or as a way of structuring the actions of the individuals involved. Sometimes it looks as though society is subsumed in the individual (e.g. Mannheim's [1969, pp.295ff] 'historically representative' figure) who impose their will upon it, but from another point of view that person's character is configured by the transcending circumstances of the situation, e.g. the emergence of Margaret Thatcher as a political agent. Althusser's later work (Elliott, 1998, pp.26-8) on conjunction or encounter contained a notion of contingency based on an argument resembling this in the important sense of seeing contingency in terms of singular figures or events as overdetermined by their broader circumstances.

Hence we can argue that while agents perceive the world as externality, as alien contingency, 'out-there', the phenomenological perspective can provide an account of how this comes about without theory removing the subject's creativity from the picture. Whilst self-interest and individualism might be seen as asocial, Merleau-Ponty's insight enables us to capture them as institutional features related to the fragmenting tendencies of modern capitalism. Hence, the pure negativity of the self-conscious ego is already institutionally mediated. Marx's image of capitalism as driven by its internal conflicts ('capitalist production begets... its own negation' (Marx, 1974, p.715) is apposite here: the contradictions do not entail the disintegration of social life (although they might bring about its transformation) nor render its elements asocial but, on the contrary, constitute their very sociality.

Power, Objectification, Types and Stereotypes

As Kruks (*op. cit.*, p.128) notes, in Merleau-Ponty's earlier work the notion of the gaze served to represent what was in effect a Hegelian notion of power relations where power is expressed in terms of the ability to fix the other's self-perception in terms of the gaze. Hence, stereotyping can be seen as the result of an imbalance of power where others emerge from a struggle between a putative pure negating subject and the subject which becomes the focus of its superior objectifying powers. More recently, Foucault's (1980) work on the operation of institutional power through networks of discourses within which subjects are fixed or subjectivised in a discursive gaze has illuminated mechanisms of power.

The work of Jessica Benjamin (1990) has also served to highlight power relations, but this time specifically in terms of a critique of Freudianism as a discourse or theoretical ideology concentrating on the intrapsychic - that which has been internalised - arguably at the expense of the on-going dynamic between subjects. She highlights the Freudian view of the mother-child relationship in which the mother appears as an object for the child (*ibid.*, pp.23-4). This can be seen as tying into wider networks of discourses which serve to fix women as mothers or otherwise into institutional complexes where a male gaze operates.

The hegemonic power of psychological ideologies has become evident through the way agency is deemed to internalise its environmental influences such that it appears as an effect of the process. The institutional processes thus seem to disappear within the individual. In this way networks of psychologically-oriented discourses freeze or suture individuals from their institutional context.

Notions of the unconscious within this field of discourse have been able to assimilate all manner of heterogeneous material in hegemonic fashion. The 'unconscious' has become a repository of forgotten, unrecognised and taken-for-granted aspects of the social world which are thus stored away as ready-to-be-utilised items rather than unobserved, on-going aspects of a social world which run intersubjectively through embodied subjects and whose collective meanings are in principle accessible to us all (Kruks, *op. cit.*, pp.119, 130). This psychologising of the everyday has the effect of opening up a gap between institution and agency and serves as a useful example of the objectifying power of institutional discourses.

We can give an illustration of this by examining the situatedness of ethnic minorities within institutional processes where we find sociologists describing the objectifying process, institutional racism. It can be argued that if we grasp the import of the phenomenological point just made then it is clear that race is not something that does or does not exist as a reality in discrete individuals but should rather be seen as related to an institutional process which fixes 'race' in individuals. In other words, the discursive gaze of institutional networks attempts to assimilate groups by 'othering' them. 'Race' is then also an objectification of a power relation as the gaze is always contested by those it attempts to 'other', if we follow Merleau-Ponty's model of 'institution'. This is an important point in that debates about race often centre on the possibility or non-possibility of locating for groups key distinguishing characteristics rather than on the institutional power relations of intersubjective communication/conflict through which such objectifications are generated. A converse situation arises where groups have the power to differentiate themselves within a context where differentiation has previously been resisted.

While it is clear that, perhaps in some sense well captured by Foucault (1980), institutional power depends on the ability to circulate meanings, the analysis of this process of dissemination of 'truths' tends to be conducted in a neo-Weberian style which fails to explain how official meanings are produced (D'Amico, 1989).[3] Perhaps most importantly this view takes bureaucracies as operating outside the more or less formal institutional frameworks of cultural life within which they are situated. The net effect is to present bureaucracies as institutions 'out-there' with their own inexorable tendencies. A graphic example of this is Bauman's account of the Holocaust.

Bauman's argument seems to be that the formal organisational structures (of modernity), once set in motion - for example, the signing of a document - produce irresistible trains of events (Bauman, 1991, pp.105-6). On the other hand, Strauss (1964) has argued that the actual working of bureaucracies and such like, is a negotiated order which involves the interpretation of formal codes against a background of unarticulated *savoir faire* through which they make sense and become operable (Worsley, 1978, pp.546-8). Hence, the neo-Weberian position mistakes ideal type models for the actual workings of organisations. Institution as sedimented praxis would therefore seem nearer the mark than viewing organisations as following their formal, ideal-typical characteristics in reality.

The 'out-there' character of bureaucracy as having fixed goals, values and conventional definitions in neo-Weberian theory of organisations highlighted by Bauman's idea of the inexorability of bureaucracy-as-set-in-motion is challenged by Strauss's view that goals are always under interpretation in the light of ever-present background assumptions about what they *actually* mean.

Following the earlier suggestions from Merleau-Ponty, it could also be argued that it would be wrong to see the bureaucracy as operating in isolation, but rather as a part of an institutional network, the weight of whose meanings bears down on any communicative practice within the organisation. This also interacts with the biographical trajectories of its agents who are at once suffused in the generality of their institutional situatedness and also uniquely positioned within it. As such, agents become the focus of general tendencies but at the same time remain negating subjectivities. This produces a conflictual dynamic whose outcome always has an element of contingency and hence openness of situation.

Further, it is possible for agents to grasp the sense or direction of events, although as suggested above this may only be at the level of 'know-how' rather than knowledge. The *'sens'* is always mediated by the overall historical situation (Kruks, *op. cit.*, pp.139, 142-3) and therefore intersubjectivity is complex and contradictory. Merleau-Ponty speaks of projects coming to an end and subjects may be operating with senses relating to such past projects rather than making a transition to the developing situation (*ibid.*, p.139). This could be exemplified in the transition from welfarism to Thatcherism, where attempts to identify what was happening in terms of the old hegemonic political culture simply failed to make sense and produced a feeling of disorientation.[4]

Hence if we are to understand subjectivity in, for example, Bauman's 'worst case' scenario of the Holocaust, it must be possible to see action as oriented by the complex mediation of institution in the individual: the historical political-juridical status of Jews in Germany, the attitude of the Jewish leadership, the everyday racism which overlaps and is interstitial with (following Strauss's methodology) every institutional action. It must further be acknowledged that although people might sense the new political settlement, they might not be able to name it. Thirdly, there is the dimension where actors are still trying to read the new situation through the grammar of the previous political culture (with its own forms of racism) and are failing to make sense of events, that is, grasp its *sens*.

Bauman's account of the Holocaust gets rid of agency (after the initial act) and events are described in terms of the autonomy of bureaucratic structures, even to the extent of producing agents who are detached from the effects of their roles (Bauman, *op. cit.*, pp.115-16). Whilst this might be *psychologically* true, it would surely be wrong to take this for an *intersubjective* hiatus, a situation where agents no longer interpret their roles. In Merleau-Ponty's terms this would be a history without *sens*.

If, on the other hand, we employ the latter's approach it is possible to see an intersection between agency and institution rather than a reduction of the former to the latter. Roles may structure actions but on the other hand roles must make sense, that is, be interpretable as part of wider structures. Merleau-Ponty (1992, pp.448-9) notes that as history 'can never be detached from us to play the role of an alien force using us for its own ends, then *precisely because it is always history lived through* we cannot withhold from it at least a fragmentary meaning'. It is therefore possible to discuss the rationality of agents (however poisonous), and to see why they did what they did via their understanding of situation.

Rationality and Ideology Critique

The neo-Weberian analysis refracted through Bauman's lens is also evident in the treatment of popular culture found in the writings of the Frankfurt School.[5] Whilst the contribution of the early Frankfurt School to understanding popular (but not high) culture as an industrial process and their characterisation of its production as routinisation and standardisation was important in revealing the economic basis of culture, that is as a production process, there was a failure to go beyond the formal meanings of cultural products, to understand how people made sense of them. The rationality at the heart of the everyday was ignored. One strand of Althusser's (1971) work on ideology also followed this route through his application of the category of 'misrecognition' to certain ways of seeing or forms of practice. However, another strand of his thinking suggested that as an everyday feature ideology was important for what it did rather than for making formal truth claims. This latter ties in with Dummett's (*op. cit.*, p.132) position that everyday, natural language utterances, function as descriptions which are also actions rather than direct truth claims; they are ways of relating to, picking out objects rather than propositions. They are ways of grasping the sense of a context in which utterances are made. The latent prepositional content can be rendered explicit via a hermeneutics of the context.

The phenomenological approach therefore offers an alternative characterisation of agency to the Bauman and Frankfurt views - which can loosely be categorised as critiques of modernity which echo the pessimism of Weber's rationalisation thesis.

As with Strauss and the ethnomethodologists, Dummett's (*op. cit.*, p.44) view is that formal linguistic codes and conventions always require interpretation before things become manageable, that is, can be negotiated, made sense of. He thus distinguishes between the sense of expressions (contextual meaning) and their significance, which consists in the coding or conventions used to indicate what is meant, a relatively ossified aspect of meaning.

Dummett's emphasis on sense and context as means of determining the rationality of communicative practices echoes Merleau-Ponty's view that

> ...our errors become truths only once they are recognised, and there remains a difference between their revealed and their latent content of truth, between their alleged and their actual significance (*ibid.*, p.398).

The implication of this for cultural critique is that the Frankfurt assessment of the untruth and manipulative character of mass culture needs to be regarded as an explanation of the last resort rather than the primary way of dealing with everyday discourse and popular culture (which may have no explicit epistemic reference) as it is premised on the view that meanings and discourses are to be treated directly according to epistemological standards. That is, for the Frankfurt School, meanings are taken to be located in the prevailing linguistic conventions of the time rather than in the actuality of the meaning context.

The Gap Between Perception and Practice in Merleau-Ponty

Kruks (*op. cit.*, pp.135-6) criticises Merleau-Ponty's failure to adjust an account of intersubjectivity based on perception to his later praxis orientation. That is, if intersubjective meanings are generated via praxis (socially self-constituting activity) then they cannot be the same, or arrived at by the same argument, as meanings derived from detached perception of an object. Here Kruks (*loc. cit.*) gives the example of two people viewing a landscape who have a similar background. in art appreciation. By contrast, in the praxis version, the intersubjective content of the interaction/ perception would depend on the degree to which subjects are situated within common projects, rather than on perception alone. And, for Merleau-Ponty, common projects contain, at the same time, the conflictual demands of situated egos. This is taken as an integral part of communicative practices (*ibid.*, p.128).

Whilst the notion of praxis incorporates a dialectic of action and cognition, Merleau-Ponty does not theorise the nature of the relationship between them. Dummett's (1981, p.132) account of natural language utterances is helpful here. It suggests that communicative understanding - which can be taken in a perceptual, everyday way - has a cognitive content which is achieved in a practical manner. That is, it is attained through common linguistic practices by which we relate to, pick out situations - structures, agents, states of affairs, events, etc. The relating is active in that it constructs the situations within the limits of meaning contexts and at the same time it has cognitive significance in that the action of relating to a situation is a way of grasping the sense of it, which is perceptually, in Merleau-Ponty's terms perhaps, an awareness of the world that flows through us.

Hence, the practical activity of relating to situations by conversing leads on to a characterising of our sense of the situation by objectifying it or picking out, identifying what is going on. Because identifying and relating are part of the same practical process for Dummett, the objects we pick out are always self-relating. This self-referentiality of our objects is not a form of circularity however, as there are different ways of picking out or objectifying the sense of a situation (*loc. cit.*). Merleau-Ponty is perhaps more explicit about this in his recognition that agents always bring a unique biographical/institutional situatedness to an encounter and their negating subjectivities as embodied in differing projects will be a consideration. It follows that situations or meaning contexts remain open-ended.

Notes

1   The volumes of particular relevance are du Gay (1997), du Gay *et al.* (1997) and Mackay (1997).

2   Giddens' (1990) references to the disembeddedness of experience are called into question here. Giddens makes an unjustifiable identification between embeddedness and the prevalence of dyadic interactions rather than acknowledging interaction as taking place with the intersubjective content of a *locale itself*.

3   D'Amico (1989, pp.101, 105-6) argues that in Foucault discursive statements are somehow objective and prior to subjectivity - or in our terms, 'out-there'. However, without subjects the production of meaning remains a mystery.

4   See, for example, Drabble (1979) in Whitehead (1985, pp.391-2) on middle class angst in the unfolding hegemonic crisis of the U.K. in the 1970s. Hines (1981) gives, as Whitehead (*loc. cit.*) also notes, an account of the development of a culture of 'mutual recrimination' in those times, confirming the loss of a *sens* (directedness) to everyday life.

5   See Adorno and Horkheimer (1989), Adorno (1991) and also Negus (1997, pp.67-118) for a general discussion of rationalisation and the 'culture industries'.

2 The Limits of the Phenomenological Perspective

In this part of the discussion we shall investigate how intersubjectivity introduces the world to us as a factor shaping or limiting our thought processes. In other words, we will ask how does the intersubjective aspect of social life avoid being merely subjective, and rather, provide a point of reference for individual subjectivity or consciousness from outside that individual perspective.

Hence this chapter will examine some notions of intersubjectivity in the hope of arriving at something distinctively intersubjective rather than formulations which reduce to what has been termed a sociology (Denzin, 1992, p.16) or philosophy (Dews, 1987, p.227) of consciousness. The latter is exemplified in the work of G.H. Mead and the symbolic interactionists wherein the relationship between an intersubjective 'generalised other' and individual consciousnesses is one in which the former is transparent to the latter and thus undermines the possibility of a non-homogenised or non-normalised, non-consensual, non-passive subjectivity. As such, it is at one with socialisation model of functionalist sociology with its emphasis on consensual order rather than emancipation and autonomy.

Similarly, despite his interest in the latter, Habermas (1991) approaches intersubjectivity via the notion of an anthropological tendency towards communicative consensus. In *The Philosophical Discourse of Modernity*, Habermas assimilates a pragmatics of communication to the work of Frege and Dummett on truth-conditional semantics. However, there are significant differences between Habermas and Frege-Dummett relevant to the present discussion. Habermas sees meaning as dependent on a consensus of communication norms given by the 'ideal speech situation' which guides the consciousness of communicants. Dummett (*op. cit.*, p.51), on the other hand, notes that for Frege in communicative understanding the senses of truth-bearing sentences exist independently of our grasping them mentally; they express a truth or reality directly, that is, without the guidance of a regulative ideal. Hence, for Frege and Dummett, the role of a judging individual subjectivity is quite distinct from the (non-mental) linguistic activity of expressing truths about the world. Wittgenstein (see below) also has argued that understanding, using language appropriately, picking out its sense, is not a mental process. Dummett (*op. cit.*, pp.25-6) himself sees intersubjective understanding as an independent domain; he stresses its ontological rather than epistemological character. Language becomes a bearer (*Bedeutung*) of thoughts rather than a means of their semantic construction. Thoughts are expressed by conversants whose sentential productions are given sense by their contextual nature. Consequently, intersubjectivity is something performed, enacted or made real through utterance rather than being consciousness or knowledge itself.

Now, following Wittgenstein's point that understanding is not a mental process and yet language is used as a 'mastery of technique' to sort things, the very way reflexivity is understood as a mirroring of the world in the mind has to be reappraised. That is, the world is 'mirrored' or picked out in the above accounts but intersubjectively rather than as conscious individual knowledge. The notion that the thought expressed by the sense of a sentential statement, itself serves as a reference (involves an ontology of meaning) is a rebuff to postmodern critics of reference who assume reference means gesturing towards a world prior to meaning, a world 'out-there'. Dummett (*op. cit.*, p.367) makes a similar point when he notes that, for Frege, objects are grasped only by means of 'the senses of expressions which could be used to refer to them' and that 'Sense determines reference' (*ibid.*, p.157). Reference exists within discourse but is not coincident with agents' meanings or objectifications. It exists in the everyday, taken for granted level of communication which interacts with agents' meanings to provide the sense or logic of situations. Thus reference does not entail subjectivised meanings or a world of objects totally constructed in discourse, but rather a framework through which individual agents can make sense of the world.

The first part of the chapter looks at communicative interaction in Mead, Schutz, Habermas and Adorno whilst the latter part views linguistic conventionalism in Rorty and Davidson through the critical lens of a phenomenology of language.

Part 1: Communicative Interaction in Social Theory

G.H. Mead: Formation of the Subject in Consciousness

According to Mead (1970, pp.173-8), the reflexive moment or 'phase' of selfhood - the 'I' - involves consciousness of the attributions, definitions, roles which are ascribed to it by others, that is to say, these are reflected in consciousness (the 'I' phase) and embodied in an experiential self which is present to consciousness. Mead refers to consciousness of this embodied aspect of selfhood as the 'me' phase of self-consciousness.

The need to grasp the transformative aspect of selfhood as one of conscious organisation and incorporation of the other is clearly understood here. The problem remains, as with traditional idealism, that one must be present to oneself in these mental operations. Although it is recognised by Mead and subsequent interactionist writers that the 'I' is of a different order of consciousness to and cannot be known in the same way as the self-ascribed contents of empirical self-consciousness they nevertheless proceed as if the 'I' is a deliberative entity, that it calculates the way roles can be successfully taken on for the accomplishment of integration in the social order defined by the other. This is both behaviouristic and contradictorily, it would seem, deliberative. Selfhood is defined in terms of dramaturgical qualities: social actors take up, rearrange, negotiate and discard roles. As Schutz (1967, p.217) observes, there is no scope here for the purely 'inner' activities of imagination and calculation which do not directly involve behavioural responses, role-taking. Schutz places this perspective within its limits - those of 'the insulated stream of consciousness of the single individual'. It is as if transactions take place between the 'I' and 'me' aspects of self where these are completely independent of any social nexus. Once internalised (Mead, *op. cit.*, p.155, f.8), the other appears to be sutured from its origins. Schutz (*op. cit.*, p.218) observes of the subject as described by Mead that it is 'as if the wide-awake man with the natural attitude [that is, with his taken for granted - H.F.] could be thought of as separate from his fellow-men'.

Clearly, the paradoxical effect of Mead's position is to present selfhood as at once passive social product ('me' phase) and transcendental, indeterminate ego ('I' phase). He does argue that the 'I' is a sedimentation of former 'me' states and in doing so implies that the 'I' is a socially determinate entity but does not theorise its links with the 'me', its *modus operandi*. For Mead, this is not an issue of the formation of self-consciousness by heterogeneous, that is, non-conscious factors, but rather a function of different levels within self-consciousness. Contrary to this, Schutz's view is that Mead's level of transcendental ego ('I') is precisely the point of social determination of consciousness rather than its ineffability, it is the point at which selfhood interpenetrates with the web of taken for granted practices and beliefs which Schutz argues arise through work, that is, practical activity, which always requires a framework of operable assumptions, a stock of knowledge, accumulated wisdom, recipe, knack. It is through such taken for granted structures that conscious thoughts receive their shape.

The reflexive process, that of 'identifying' connections or 'thought objects', goes ahead, on Schutz's account without identification in the classical sense taking place, that is, without the *conscious* categorisation of data (roles, practices etc.). For example, a person may say 'In that situation I would do this' but yet be unable to identify classes of such situations or actions.

Now if reflexivity is not regarded as a process of knowing in this Meadian subject-centred sense of identifying actions, roles etc. as being of a certain sort, it is still one which nevertheless orders representations by making spontaneous connections between them. Hence the crucial function of reflexivity is maintained in this modified version: that is, the function of connecting whatever is represented to the self with individual consciousness, cognition. However, unlike the traditional view, here the performance of tasks is not dependent on a consciousness of them. This, it is argued, explains how people perform competently in social situations despite a lack of knowledge of the processes involved. It is not claimed that people cannot become conscious of their taken for granted social assumptions, but rather that this involves 'unconsciously' replacing the excavated set of 'natural attitudes' with another 'taken for granted'.

The development of Schutz's views in the ethnomethodology of Harold Garfinkel (1967) and others sees the elaboration of the natural attitude in terms of 'indexicality' and 'reflexivity'. These two processes operate together to generate meaning. Indexing or referring is a property of language - one is able to grasp what is referred to even where no explicit reference is made; however this only works because of the reflexive ability to pick out the relevant situations and correct the indexing where it is inappropriate (Garfinkel, *op. cit.*, p.4).

Mead (*op. cit.*, pp.152-6) and other interactionists such as Goffman (1982) write as if 'taking the role of the other', that is, picking out appropriate actions, situations, etc. were a fully conscious, deliberative process of identifying or classifying these and adopting them. They are unable to account for the limits to appropriate situational moves which in Schutz and ethnomethodology are demarcated by the contents of the taken for granted of the natural attitude - which provides the logic of the situation. This sense of how roles should be applied is missing in Meadian internalisation which sees the generalised other (*loc. cit.*) as an inventory of 'right' roles at the back of our consciousness. In theoretical terms, this individualisation of the generalised other leads to a sense of solipsistic ignorance about what is appropriate to the other as the materials the Meadian subject has to construct its role-playing from are, so to speak, already 'all in the mind' of the individual subject itself.

Schutz: The Natural Attitude and the Taken for Granted

Now Schutz's insight of the 'natural attitude' prevents such a reduction of the world to the contents of an individual consciousness. It helps to explain how it is that agents grasp the limits of types of action, 'know' when they are moving on from one kind of situation to another, and to sense where the current response ceases to be appropriate. This ability to negotiate reality cannot be fully explained in terms of a deliberative attitude such as is found in Goffman's (1968) view that roles serve as masks behind which individuals maximised their room for manoeuvre. Rather it makes sense to see it in terms of *what deliberation is about*; what is grasped in consciousness is something irreducibly other than consciousness. In Garfinkel's case then, consciousness may or may not grasp the situations which the natural attitude reflexively picks out via 'knack', 'technique', '*savoir faire*'. Hence theoretical understanding implies a division of labour between a reflexive picking out of the object, in other words, a spontaneous *intersubjective* understanding of what is required in a situation and giving an account of this situation in propositional terms. Conversely, for Garfinkel (*op. cit.*, p.4), reflexivity stabilises meaning and communication and thus provides a framework of common assumptions, a shared world of meanings which demarcates the limits of the object of the theoretical account. Hence, this taken for granted 'background' is the substructure within which knowledge of the object can be produced.

The Everyday World as Already-Constructed Types of Practical Activity

Following Husserl's notion that the empirical world of the everyday is always already categorialised (see Chapter 6), Schutz (*op. cit.*, p.6) argues that it is the 'already-constructed' aspect of action/decision which proves fundamental in explaining it. He argues that human beings have pre-selected and pre-interpreted the social world via

> a series of common sense constructs of the reality of daily life, and it is these thought objects which determine their behaviour, define the goal of their action, and the means...in brief which help them to find their bearings within their environment and to come to terms with it.

Common sense is not only an attribute of popular thinking but also of science; in fact *every* practice has its taken for granted basis (*loc. cit.*). Schutz argues that the social world itself is structured in terms of constructs which enable us to make sense of it. The constructs embody rules which facilitate the process of classifying social action (*ibid.*, p.14). In terms of the received (Cartesian) way of addressing the world there is a constitutive ambiguity about Schutzian constructs or thought objects in that they have both 'mental' and physical aspects; they are ideas which only exist insofar as they are performed. This theme will be investigated in Chapter 6.

Schutz claims that the constructs are necessary to explain how it is that many of the things we do are done habitually. We suppress from consciousness, or do not know the primary factors in some practice:

> we apply the construction...in following recipes and rules of thumb which have stood the test so far and in frequently stringing together means and ends without clear knowledge 'about' their real connections (*ibid.*, p.21).

Hence, although it is impossible to account for rule-following on the paradigm of rational thinking

> ...we receive reasonable answers to reasonable questions...we perform in factories and laboratories and offices highly 'rationalised' activities, we play chess together...How is this possible?' (*ibid.*, p.32).

In fact, 'neither the origin or import' of these rules is rationally understood in common sense thinking. Schutz concludes that 'rational action' on a common sense level is always action within a background of an 'unquestioned and undetermined frame of constructs of typicalities' of the situation and its participants (*ibid.*, p.33).

Schutz bases the distinction he makes here between different types of understanding on William James's division between 'knowledge by acquaintance' and 'knowledge about' (*ibid.*, p.1). Common sense is like the former. It operates with a system of typifications of the sort described above through which private experiences are transformed into a communicable content (*ibid.*, p.12).

Schutz notes that the

> typifying medium par excellence...is the vocabulary and the syntax of everyday language...The pre-scientific vernacular can be interpreted as a treasure-house of ready-made pre-constituted types and characteristics, all socially derived and carrying along an open horizon of unexplored content (*ibid.*, p.10).

Like Gramsci (see Chapter 3), Schutz argues that the way we ordinarily make sense of things is via a culturally *sedimented* structure of interpretation. The knowledge that supersedes the thought objects of private knowledge of the world 'has its history, it is a part of our "social heritage"...' (*ibid.*, p.13).

Because Schutz's notion of a typified knowledge falls closer to 'acquaintance knowledge' than 'knowledge about' the construct is hence not the same as a fully fledged classificatory system. Its open horizon of unexplored content suggests it is not a closed (self-identical) conceptual system, but a capacity for multiple interpretations. The fact that constructs are not abstractions but wedded to real situations indicates the performative quality of this knowledge.

The 'We-Relationship': Constructs and Intersubjectivity

The taken for granted shared rules provide a specific form of consciousness for Schutz, 'we-consciousness'. 'We-consciousness' not only enables subjects to experience a shared world but also makes it possible to pick out objects, to entertain the particularity of the everyday world. The reflexive quality of situations is denoted in that we can see them as part of our biography; we can see ourselves in them. The fact that the world is experienced, following Husserl, in the mode of typicality, does not debar us from entertaining the uniqueness of things (*ibid.*, p.59).

Schutz argues that our idea of uniqueness is framed by the way various typicalities are conjoined. For example, Rover, his Irish setter, is a conjunction of the typicalities 'Irish Setter', 'dog', 'mammal', 'animal', 'organism' or 'object of the outer world'. Hence Schutz observes, 'The unique objects and events given to us in a unique aspect are unique within a horizon of typical familiarity' (*loc. cit.*). In other words, the individual's horizon of constructs structures the way these intersubjective categories come together. For example, my view of Rover is given by the way these typicalities are fused in a specific biography. Schutz goes on to say that what is considered to be unique is a matter of interest, relevance or problem at hand. In other words, the intentionality of our biography, our mode of practice, projects and so on, represents a particular conjunction of typicalities or forms of action.

The significance of this point for characterising intersubjectivity is simply that Rover, for instance, is not grasped as a series of generic Chinese boxes 'Irish Setter', 'dog', 'mammal' etc., that is, not abstractly, but only in relation to my biography. My conception of Rover is a *situated* knowledge; Rover is part of my history, not a feature of propositions about dogs in general.

The crux of our discussion here is Schutz's recognition of the open-endedness of the taken for granted structures of thought; the fact that they are based on typicality which underlies and confers meaning on the categories employed by the classifying subject.

The 'we-relationship', Schutz notes, is a state of consciousness which is different from the self-consciousness of the individual subject. Rather, it is a totalised state of consciousness in which the consciousness of all those with some interaction with an individual's biography is contained. The contribution of the individual to that consciousness is 'bracketed' within this, following Husserl. Again, as with Husserl, this 'we-consciousness' is a kind of transcendental ego or consciousness, and indeed also seems to bear some similarity in its regulative capacity to the notion of the internalised 'generalised other' embodied in Mead's notion of the self.

Now for Schutz, there is still a problem of what is not embodied in the typical constructs of we-consciousness. In other words, there is still a private area of consciousness, the terrain of the non-typical. Hence at the level of typical constructs, I cannot fully understand what the other means. Consequently, for Schutz, unlike Frege (Dummett, *op. cit.*, pp.58-6) the objective status of meaning is problematic. Schutz (*op. cit.*, p.57) refers to the lack of interest in and satisfactory solution to the problem of knowledge of other minds, and hence of intersubjectivity, as a 'scandal of philosophy'.

One objection that might be made at the outset to Schutz's account is to viewing the operation of constructs as a *mental* process. This means that self and Other have to be differentiated as that which belongs to my mind and that which belongs to the Other. It is suggested here that a we-consciousness cannot operate on the terrain of selves and Others. The reference to Others actually presupposes the task of we-consciousness; that is it presumes already formed selves through the work of self-recognition. To say that there are selves and Others operating in the domain of the taken for granted is assuming that what the constructs do - create identities - is already accomplished! It follows that the idea that we-consciousness involves some kind of transcendence of self-consciousness, and the claim that in this process there is some residue of self lost to the public domain, are both incoherent. The taken for granted provides an infrastructure for the conscious articulation of theories or propositions about everyday life. As such, it would seem to be the framework within which recognition of selves as owners of action or motive constructs can occur. Hence, to ascribe self-recognition at the level of the social world in which selves are being synthesised out of actions and motives seems to be doing violence to the grammar of self-ascription. For example, Schutz (*op. cit.*, p.15) notes: '...in daily life I construct types of the Other's field of acquaintance...I assume that he will be guided by certain relevant structures...' etc.

The issue of how it is that people manage to operate without consciously thinking through all their actions and how this impinges on what consciousness is will be reviewed later through some comments on Wittgenstein and Dummett.

Critical Theory and the Circle of Self-Consciousness

The problem of the formation of self-identity is taken up within critical theory by Adorno and Habermas in particular. Adorno attacks the paradoxes mentioned above in terms of the notion of a 'non-identical self', a self not constrained by consciousness, whose content is seen as mediating, and thus preserving the objectivity of the concept formation from a position of non-identical subjectivity beyond it. Adorno (1973, pp. 162-6) illustrates what it might be like to think in this way. He argues that the theoretical work of Marx and Weber might be considered as consisting of ideal types whose contents are never fully classified in terms of conceptual hierarchies but rather overlap and work by association, the constellation of ideas which surround and is structured by the concept rather than being enclosed within it. A similar line of investigation is pursued by the early Feuerbach (1986, p.65) who argued that the world intersects the concept (the conscious subject) rather than being encircled by it.

As Dews (1987, p.226) observes, neither of these manoeuvres is fully elaborated as a way of showing how conscious thought can mediate truth or objectivity. Habermas (1980), on the other hand, in a Kantian turn, makes the regulative structures of communication represent the 'outside' of conscious thought processes. The characterisation of such structures as aiming at ideal speech situations rather than expressing a reality as such, means that the objects denoted in this *Diskurs* are only approximations to those identified by the transcending ideal situation. Distortion occurs in the communicative process due to its siting within historically determinate kinds of repressive contexts, but, none the less, conversants are guided by a transcendental regulative structure occasioned by the necessary conditions for communicative competence. These conditions transcend any actual content but are linked to the content as they necessarily mediate it and thus provide its link with objectivity.

Now Habermas sacrifices the Husserlian empirical reality of the world of preconstituted types but recaptures it via the structures of communication. These prove to be socio-historically determinate and hence guarantee the social determination of knowledge. They provide a redefinition of the life-world where intersubjectivity includes propositionally-oriented communication or *Diskurs*. Arguably, the abandonment of the pre-given world of typifications and its natural language format is a mistake as it represents that which is external to consciousness, the sedimentation of the subjective in the world, the self-referencing of reality by the description which is inseparable from the practice; the utterance as 'doing'. As Garfinkel (1967, p.1) notes, 'accounts' in everyday life are an 'accomplishment...and are made to happen as events...that in organising they describe'. Garfinkel's point could be illustrated by the examples 'I am shopping for...', 'Let me show you what I mean', or 'You have framed this discussion succinctly'. This is further discussed in Chapter 7.

Habermas (1991, pp.312-3) takes Frege's truth conditional semantics, which theorises the relationship between propositional language and the (intersubjective) world of interaction, as a basis for his account of intersubjectivity. Separate assumptions are introduced which go against the

Fregean position. Intersubjectivity and objectivity are seen as separate domains and the intersubjective world entertains knowledge ('validity') claims. However, the claims made by subjects about the status of their communications are clearly not part of natural language in Dummett's account of Frege. Natural language expresses a state of affairs and as such is part of the world, not a comment on it. Its reflexivity is spontaneous or natural, rather than calculated. Hence like Husserl, Schutz *et al.*, it takes the world to be self-referential, already constituted symbolically. The Habermasian knowledge claims undermine the objective status of natural language (as expressing a state of affairs) given in the Frege-Dummett view. Consequently, Habermas's self-conscious subject is reincorporated into the terrain of the lifeworld which in Husserl is supposed to guarantee the objectivity of communication (although this can only be expressed propositionally through the work of a transcendental consciousness). Thus, 'Participants draw from this lifeworld...the background knowledge from which propositional contents are fed' (*ibid.*, p.31). Communication is split into a subjective part in which speakers interact and an objective zone pertaining to 'objects or states of affairs *concerning* which they seek agreement' (Dews, *op. cit.*, p.238). In contrast, the Frege-Dummett view is that communication expresses states of affairs etc. even where sentences are non-propositional. The thoughts expressed in a statement which satisfies truth conditions are at the same time real entities. Hence the world is not something separate from communication. Gadamer (1981, p.95) describes Habermas's position as one in which

> linguistic understanding [is] interpreted in a very limited way...as a sort of closed circle of the movement of ideas, as the cultural heritage of a people divorced from their everyday living.

Further, Gadamer notes, whilst Habermas acknowledges that labour, domination, ideals of liberty and order exist outside language,

> One would want to admit rather that every linguistic experience of the world is experience of the world, not experience of language. And is what we articulate in language not an encounter with reality? (*loc. cit.*).

Habermas's focus on matching propositions concerning content of utterances with those designating agreement about the content (Dews, *loc. cit.*) seems to be at the expense of engaging the world which propositions formulate and points away from the everyday and into a circle of subject-centred reason.

The consequence is that Habermas has to treat subjectivity and intersubjectivity as undifferentiated and cannot account for the natural reflexivity of rule-following which acts as a guide to concept formation as in the case of Schutz's Irish Setter. It also drives a wedge between language and practice which Schutz's notion of constructs as recipes, rules of thumb overcomes through communication as doing. Here the successful practical engagement with the world is that of 'describing', figuring, its outlines.

In Schutz's 'we-consciousness', as with Habermas, there is a failure to separate out the functions of intersubjectivity from those of subjectivity, but, importantly, Schutz recognises the *preconstituted*, open nature of the life world constructs. Now if, as Habermas suggests, these are organised as knowledge claims (propositions), then they are circumscribed within individual subjectivity as that individual's claim over its own mental contents. The nature of the proposition is that it classifies or represents aspects of the world in the form 'A is a case of B' following the underlying classificatory rule 'if there is anything such that it is A then it is a case of B'. The problem with classification is that it goes against the world in the sense that it prioritises and also excludes aspects for the purposes of its own project. And, ironically, as Adorno (1973, pp.162-3) notes, it is constituted by what it excludes; the concept (classification system) depends for its identity on the constellation of ideas it forbids, its mediation by its non-identity. Adorno's point that conceptual meanings are determined by associated but excluded meanings will be pursued in a different way through linguistics (denotation and connotation) in Chapters 4 and 5. The gist of such open meaning can however be gathered from the following representation of the contrast between typical construct (associative) and conceptual meaning.

Figure 2.1 suggests how forms of thought can organise ideas without the activity of naming, that is, identifying, as described above taking place.[1] The openness of typical constructs is indicated where there is a possibility that the centrality of one idea might be shifted by additional connections which are apprehended later with regard to any of the peripheral ideas.[2] However, in Figure 2.2, B, F, E and D are definitionally instances of A, and even if the centre of gravity shifts due to A being definitionally subsumed under some more general category Z, it still remains true that the other ideas are subsumed under A.

In applying these models to subjectivity, the subsumption of experiences or thoughts under a self (A), as required in self-consciousness, necessitates the model in Figure 2.2. Yet the notion of typicality represented in 2.1 does not allow for this kind of closure. In 2.2 however, it is not logically possible that the experiences could be someone else's, nor is it possible that I have them without identifying them as mine. Hence the thought or experience becomes merely subjective. In the left-hand case, it is possible that I have them without consciously ascribing them to myself; here the self (A) though centrally configured, appears as one thought amongst others and hence displaceable by something interrelating and reconfiguring all these elements. Hence A appears here as a part of a common discourse of thoughts not subject to the privacy of individual ownership and therefore not merely subjective.

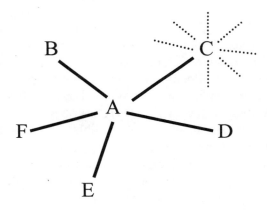

Figure 2.1: Open Semantic System: the Typical Construct

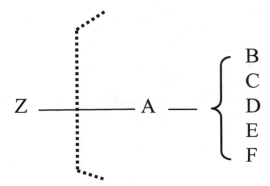

Figure 2.2: Semantic Closure via Conceptual Classification

Now the problem for Schutz, and 'interactionism' in general, is that the debate about connecting, identifying, naming, grasping, sensing, apperceiving etc.; in other words reflexive activity of a subject, is its circumscription by the tenet that subjectivity is ultimately private. Hence the tensions in the usage of the term 'subjectivity', that is, even if what the subject takes on board is an objective reflection of the world, it still remains somehow subjective and enmeshed with private, purely individual concerns.

As McDowell (1994, pp.18-20) has pointed out, the opposite, Wittgensteinian position that experience belongs to the public realm, is equally problematic. This is because the latter view ignores the particularity of experience and consequently renders it as something constructed out of public conventions with no reference point, world-based features beyond them. Current discourse theories encounter similar problems in characterising subjectivity (cf. Chapter 6). McDowell's point is that although Wittgenstein is right about the publicness of language, our concepts and meanings are conditioned by the individually situated nature of our relation to the world. Therefore they are not exactly the same as others' concepts, but this is not a problem as meaning ultimately rests on ostensive definition, that is, showing, demonstrating to others what we mean. This of course brings us back to typicalities because, as Schutz argues, it is by understanding the taken for granted typicalities used by others that we can grasp their meaning.

The idea of typicality however, goes against the grain of the public-private dichotomy examined above and suggests its redundancy. What is typical cannot by definition be the property of individual subjects. It seems necessary, therefore, to give up the idea that reflexion of the Other takes place within the domain of individual consciousness/subjectivity and to seek some alternative formulation of reflexive subjectivity.[3] The mechanisms of intersubjectivity encased in Schutz's taken for granted seem to do the work of delineating a reflexive social world, but the Schutzian notion of subjectivity remains enmired in the logic of self-recognition possessed by the *individual* subject which is associated with subject-centred accounts of reason or knowledge.

Giddens's Criticisms of Schutz

Phenomenological social theory, according to Giddens, contains a number of confusions and reproduces the traditional dualisms, firstly, between language/thought and action and secondly, between the individual and their social environment, which Schutz attempts to circumvent. Practical activity is somehow extra discursive, then there is a discursive but non-propositional sphere and lastly a propositional sphere, which taken all in all reproduce the kind of divisions evident in Habermas's programme of interaction, *Diskurs* and so on. The phenomenological claim that the world is always already typified escapes Giddens (1979, p.73, 198, p.17) who sees everyday speech as subjective, as typifications are made purely by individual subjects rather than in intersubjective processes. Giddens's own solution to the stocks of knowledge/typifications is that they are stored in the unconscious or in people's memory traces.

This disregards a key component of phenomenological theory which is that this knowledge is also *doing*, a highly public rather than mental matter. As Wittgenstein noted (see below), everyday understanding is not part of the individual's private psyche but fully operationalised knowledge.

Giddens (1973, p.73) also argues that because everyday knowledge is contextualised rather than propositional, it must be localised - using that term in the sense of small-scale interaction. It is clear however that the contexts of phenomenological knowledge could be very general.[4] Schutz, for example, talks about the taken for granted basis of the most generalising activity, scientific practice itself. The 'everyday' is not confined to commuting or housework.

However, the points about localisation and individualisation of practical knowledge are deployed by Giddens to suggest that markets are a general feature of social life in late modernity. Individuals possess tacit knowledge through which they organise their desires and preferences. This knowledge is dispersed amongst different localities that circumscribe a subject's daily interactions. It follows that any attempt to engage in economic planning will come up against the problem of atomised, and therefore socially incalculable, preferences. This argument can be seen against the critical points made above and it is also worth noting in criticism of Giddens that in the Britain of the 1990s preferences have been *commonly* characterised, that is, in terms of a *public mood*, which is denoted in terms of the absence of a 'feelgood factor', rather than atomised desires.

It is worth turning briefly to Wittgenstein (1989), whose comments on grasping the connections or grammar of language offer a model for dealing with the interrelations of social life in general. How is it, for example, that we can successfully grasp the sense of expressions in different contexts? Wittgenstein's response was that such processes *are not mental processes* although they are forms of *understanding* (*Philosophical Investigations*, 1, 15). For Wittgenstein, to understand a language does not entail that we know all the moves that can be made in that language in advance of using them. Rather, 'to understand a language means to be master of a technique' (*ibid.*, 1,199)

This does not distinguish between situations where one grasps truth conditions of linguistic expressions and where one does not and hence lies open to the charge of conventionalism, that is, that understanding amounts to no more than grasping linguistic conventions rather than a substantive content expressed by them. Consequently, as Dummett (1981, p.6) observes, for realists, this remains an unsatisfactory formulation of understanding. The distinctions Dummett wants to make can be illustrated as follows. I can converse successfully with others by letting the context pick out the sense of the utterance :'X got out of the wrong side of the bed this morning'. The statement conveys a state of affairs whether or not it can be expressed in terms of propositions about the psychological predispositions of X. What, in the latter case, is to give the sense expressed in it an objective dimension? The only solution, Dummett (*op. cit.*, p.5) argues, is to confer upon the sense of the sentence an objectivity independent of its being grasped in a mental act.

In general, then one can say about the discursivity of social situations that people behave appropriately by sensing the meanings of situations; they apply truth conditions (or perhaps, more strictly, sense connections or limits in the reality of thought), without mentally grasping that this is so.

Part 2: Linguistic Conventionalism and the Frege-Dummett Critique

Richard Rorty and Self-Affirming Edification

We have already encountered the idea that identities are formed in a closed circle of consciousness (individual subjectivity) through the work of Mead on the generalised Other and via Habermas's notion of *Diskurs*. There was no convincing theorisation of how the linguistic process itself might be regarded as non-homologous with consciousness, that is, as a material force, although the work of Schutz (following Husserl) was seminal in raising the point that all conscious activity required a substructure of taken for granted activity, or, in Garfinkel's (1967, p.4) phrase, 'essential reflexivity'.

The postmodern pragmatism of Richard Rorty follows in the tradition of Mead in discounting any realm which may pose limits to the conversation and hence also falls prey to the 'hermeneutic circle', namely, that whatever is encountered in conversation is also circumscribed by the categories of the knowing subject and hence irremediably subjectivised.

It was argued above that the taken for granted reflexivity or non-cognitive basis of practices provided a guarantee of openness and we will turn firstly to look at how openness is handled in Rorty's 'post-pragmatism' by situating him in relation to the work of Gadamer.

Rorty and Gadamer

Rorty assimilates himself to Gadamer's (1981) theory of understanding in which a person gains understanding within a cultural tradition. That is, the experience of the tradition (*Erlebnis*) is a process through which the individual becomes cultured or enlightened (*Gebildete*) as that person's cultural horizons interact with those of other traditions. Such interaction produces a fusion of horizons (*op. cit.*, p.273 ff, p.337 ff) in which the individual's understanding is broadened. The enrichment of perspective depends on a suspension of one's own cognitive claims and an opening out to the claims of the other. The postulates of the other must be taken at face value in order to fuse with one's own in a way which averts closure in the Hegelian   manner.   Warnke   (1987,   p.165)   describes   this   as   a 'deabsolutised...conception of negation' where understanding takes place without one position or term of this dialectic superimposing itself on the other.

Now Rorty's idea of edification similarly suggests a conversation between different cultures through which we can 'foster an awareness of different possibilities of coping with the world, of new life-options and, indeed, of new modes of self-description' (cited in Warnke, *op. cit.*, p.157). However, whilst in Gadamer the function of communication is to integrate different perspectives and thus provide greater knowledge and self-foundation for the conversants, for Rorty its importance lies not in 'the possession of truths' but in our own self-development and recognition of the cultural provincialism of our own ways of thinking (*loc. cit.*). Hence our philosophical examination of theoretical activities amounts to no more than a mode of detachment: 'of seeing how different ways of making things hang together hang together' (*ibid.*, p.164).

Whilst this would seem to indicate a stance of openness as detachment, the view from Gadamer suggests that openness involves commitment. This is so in the double sense that we are committed both to the broadening of knowledge in our understandings and also, following Aristotle, to the view that our theoretical activities should reflect practical needs. Gadamer follows Husserl's notion that theoretical activity involves 'giving an account' of the everyday world and is hence guided and *limited* by the world of practical reason.

Rorty, on the other hand, wants to reject any mode of ordering thoughts in terms of some notion of epistemological validity, such as the Husserlian anchorage of truth in the everyday world or Gadamer's own insight of the fusion of horizons as a broadening of knowledge.

The Rortean opening onto new experiences characterises the edifying philosopher as one who as well as

> having kept alive the historicist sense of our beliefs also has the relativist sense that the latest vocabulary...may...be just another of the potential infinity of vocabularies in which the world can be described (Rorty, 1979, p.367).

In other words, Gadamer's logic of synthesis is matched by Rorty's implication of *choice* between discrete multiple vocabularies. The choice one makes precludes rather than fuses with or articulates others. Here, subjectivities would be cut off from each other by the syntax of choice and its 'either-or-ism'. Rorty's liberal pluralism turns out to be one of mutually uncomprehending monadic subjects.

Again, whilst both Rorty and Gadamer stress the anchorage of intellectuals in traditions, Rorty (Warnke, *op. cit.*, pp.195-6) sees the function of trying out new ideas, ways of looking at things as a means of defending the tradition rather than a genuine transformation indicated by a fusion of horizons via suspension of one's own beliefs. In the latter case there is no predetermined outcome, whilst for Rorty the purpose of the conversation is *manifestly* pre-given.

Rorty (1982, p.173) sees the position of 'Western' intellectuals as determining that truth is 'whatever emerges from the conversation of Europe'. Rorty admits that this is 'frankly ethnocentric'. Interestingly enough, Habermas (see below), starting from *a priori* criteria of rationality, ends with a similar position. For Rorty there is no transcendental principle. Rather we should embrace the Western liberal intellectual tradition, he suggests with some circularity, because it is the best way of coping that we thus far know. Warnke (*op. cit.*, p.153) observes that there is no way of distinguishing this form of allegiance to 'the West' from a 'frankly irrational' and 'frankly ethnophobic' view.

One of the problems issuing from terms such as 'Western', 'liberal', 'Europe', 'individualism' is the false homogeneity they produce. These terms do not operate primarily at a propositional level, even amongst liberal intellectuals although (*pace* Rorty) the polysemic resonances go unheeded. One clear difficulty with homogeneity manifestly resides in the pragmatist tradition itself, as exemplified in Mead. Mead's fusion of German idealism and American pragmatism subverts, at least at the programmatic level, the culture of individualism with which pragmatism coexists. The permeability of self and Other in Mead's generalised Other goes against the grain of the self-sufficient economic individual.

In Gadamerian terms, there is a kind of bogus quality to the assertion of Western intellectual self-sufficiency, and following Warnke's point about ethnophobia, this also applies to the ensuing implicit claim to superiority. Gadamer's methodology suggests the possibility of on-going fusions of viewpoint between traditions which would make a nonsense of the idea of a *purely* 'Western' worldview.

Rorty, Davidson and Reference

Rorty's eclecticism is illustrated by his claim to allegiance with the perspective of the U.S. philosopher of language Donald Davidson. Davidson (1984, pp.215-26) rejects the notion that propositions can be tested directly against the world and concludes that a first order view of reference should be abandoned as it is only when propositions have been systemically assembled that they can convey a coherent referential meaning. However, as Farrell (1994, p.119) argues, the consequence of this for Davidson is not relativism because it leaves in play the intelligibility of communication, which relates to a second order type of reference. That is, communication is only predicable on the basis that communicants are engaged in some mutually grasped concern; there is a quality of *aboutness* in their interactions.

However, Rorty (1986, p.353) is preoccupied with Davidson's reservations about first order reference which appear to allow a foothold for linguistic relativism. As Farrell (*op. cit.*, p.120) notes, at this level reference works (the world is identifiable) by means of matching descriptions against a canon of scientifically approved propositions in the course of practical investigation. This seems to approximate to a conventionalist view of scientific research,

> ...nothing counts as justification unless by reference to what we already accept, and there is no way to get outside our beliefs and our language so as to find some test other than coherence.

observes Rorty (1979, p.178), and Davidson agrees.[5]

Davidson's view here (and Rorty's) has much in common with the Vienna Circle positivists' idea that truth claims were justified by matching them against 'protocol sentences' produced by scientists, or in Neurath's terms, scientists from one's 'culture circle' (Russell, 1965a, pp.139-40). On this view of justification, Russell (*op. cit.*, p.139) observes that if we want to know what Neurath says on p.364 we need to ask the scientists of our culture circle rather than decide what Neurath says via our own 'perceptive experience'. In other words, when we regard something as true or meaningful we imply that it fits the broader cultural descriptions. The *reductio ad absurdum* of this would be that 'empirical truth can be determined by the police' (*loc. cit.*). Regarding this 'attempt to make the linguistic world self-sufficient', Russell (*op. cit.*, p.141) concludes in a way that has a contemporary resonance:

> The verbalist theories of some modern philosophers forget the homely practical purposes of everyday words...I seem to hear them saying "in the beginning was the Word", not "in the beginning was what the word means".

So, for Davidson and Rorty, sentences placed in context and within the semantic field of a comprehensive theory will map out the features of reality. The theory will locate features of the world because they are implicit in ordinary descriptions (Farrell, *op. cit.*, p.122).

Dummett: Semantic Closure Versus Semantic Context

Now, whilst in Davidson the meaning of everyday language is determined by a semantic context, Dummett (*op. cit.*, pp.459-60) argues that this ignores the role of the relation *between* items of sentential structure in the production of the sense of the sentence. The sense 'mediates between the semantic features': between the 'structure' and the 'references of its constituents' on the one hand and 'the actual employment of the sentence', on the other. The thought expressed by the sentence is therefore dependent on an ability to apply the references to some state of affairs. The notion of performance implicit here indicates a view of communication as passing beyond a formal or logicist comparison of sentences to a conception of language as 'doing'. In this way Dummett's position breaks out of the closed circle Russell identifies with Neurath.

The notion of reference cannot be discarded, Dummett (*op. cit.*, p.461) argues, as 'we cannot explain what it is to treat a name as standing for an object of a certain kind without explaining what it is to identify an object of that kind'. For example, to employ the proposition 'The Y in the box is of the type X' involves making connections of the form 'this is an X'. All language ultimately falls back on this use of demonstratives or indexicals:

> even when the proper name is capable of occurring in recognition statements, the account of the relation of reference...involves a description of the use of the most basic layer of language.

In other words, some context is always implicit if we are to make sense of statements including 'this', 'here', 'it', and so on. Hence for Dummett, reference does not work according to a crude interpretation of the causal theory of reference where it is a matter of discovering whether a 'relation obtains between a proper name and an object'. Rather, it depends on the 'context principle', that is, 'what speakers would recognize as settling the truth of sentences containing the name'. In other words, reference depends on *how* they agree on applying the name; this will determine what gets picked out by it.

There are clear parallels here with the work of Husserl, Schutz and Garfinkel. The role of demonstratives is akin to the already mentioned notion of taken for granted reflexivity. Speakers can pick out states of affairs using the demonstrative or indexical mode which depends on context of utterance. Here, the notion of reference is indissolubly linked to that of performative context. Dummett's point is that the generalising capacities of a propositional utterance depend finally on this way of recognising examples of a type of something. The propositional cannot be divorced from the contextual and indexical. Garfinkel (1967, p.4) has likewise noted the incomplete substitutability of cognitive for indexical expressions in any practical activity. The effect of this insight is to undermine the linguistic dualism which treats all language as either meaningful and propositional or as metaphorical, as action, emotive, 'everyday' and unmeaningful.

Now Rorty (1991, p.163) follows Davidson (1979, p.30ff) along this latter route, that is, everyday language, language as *used*, is deemed to be separate from cognitive, that is, propositional language. Cognitive language bears meanings whilst metaphorical, natural language only produces a cognitive effect, and is not meaningful in itself. It would be easy to slip into a debate for or against metaphorical meaning, but Dummett's position allows us to see this as a blind alley. For Dummett, metaphoricity (natural speech) is always linked at some point to an explicit univocal assertion, that is, propositional language which in turn allows unique situations to be picked out unequivocally. Russell (1965a, p.135) makes the same point when he says that although Neurath and Hempel want to ground science in public impersonal propositions the result is less than the sum of the work of private scientific knowledges. The public science is a construction involving use of *opinion* to pick out what should be included in a public science. In other words, the public science is an *account* of knowledges not in the public domain and hence is itself anchored in meanings not derivable from the propositions alone. The encyclopaedist of science thus employs taken for granted knowledge of the form 'This is what public science is'.

Rorty deploys his emphasis on purely propositional language, a language of conventional meanings, against feminists and other radicals whose discourses, he argues (1989, p.65), are not conventional, that is, cognitive, but rather, metaphorical and hence literally meaningless; their aims are mythic rather than capable of realisation.[6] For the reasons outlined above this 'strategy of marginalisation' is unconvincing.

In the field of poststructural linguistics, Derrida also has criticised the postulate of a conventional language.[7] Deconstruction lays bare the metaphorical basis of the concept (cognition). However, Derrida's (1974) own position issues from the play of difference between conventional terms and is unable to account for the stability of meaning through which speakers grasp a state of affairs à la Frege and Dummett.

Similarly, it is evident from Foucault's (1971, pp.9-11) 'orders of discourse', that he understands 'discourse' as a conventional, official kind of language, or, in Garfinkel's terms, 'objective language'. This notion lacks the phenomenological sense of language as practice, where language fulfils a double function of both describing and being what is described; of being action and also an account of action which Garfinkel (*op. cit.*, p.4) calls its essential reflexivity.

This constitutive ambiguity of natural language as meaning and action is evident in Frege's characterisation of sense as both cognitive and spatial (Dummett, *op. cit.*, p.58). An interesting discussion of sense is found in Empson (1985, pp.291, 303-5), who notes the constitutive tension between sense as in 'the senses' (spatial/physical) and the notion of sense as cognitive which is mediated by a common sense (demonstrative) understanding. Dummett's own understanding of sense privileges the ontological over the epistemological aspect of meaning (Carl, 1994, p.83). Understanding or communication between speakers is first of all an ontological matter from which cognition emerges, although like Empson, he sees sense as mediated by the semantic content of the structure of statements, expressions and sentences (*ibid.*, p.461). However, 'To speak of the identification of an object...presupposes a way of picking out the object for which no further question of identification arises' (*ibid.*, p.143). Thus, Dummett claims that placing objects within some cognitive grid depends on a prior agreement between conversants on how to do this. This agreement indicates a transparency between language users in their logic (*ibid.*, p.134) and hence arguably, a fusion of individual subjects as an intersubjective subject.

Some patterns are discernible from this discussion of communicative interaction. In some ways Habermas, Rorty and Davidson line up together; roughly this amounts to a dualistic attitude to knowledge, theory, cognition, meaning on the one side which is counterposed to interaction, performance, use, causal efficacy. It also represents a dichotomy between will, need, desire, the context and action-driven metaphorical expression and the abstract contemplation of conventional or propositional meaning. Phenomenologists and Dummett on the other hand, line up in various ways against it and arguably, provide a way of breaking out of the circle of self-confirming meanings.

Notes

[1]   The point here is that in the subject-centred view of reason or knowledge the self-conscious subject operates like the pure conceptual hierarchy; it contains knowledge as in a series of widening Chinese boxes. By contrast, the typical construct view acknowledges self-consciousness or consciousness generally as an aspect of reason but argues that the concepts are always situated or framed by an environment of practised typical constructs.

[2]   Figure 2.1 indicates that the self is displaced as the centre of ideational formation. For example, an ideology can link the self into a wider field of connections whose configurational centre is elsewhere. The self may be positioned or 'subjectivised' by patriarchal or liberal individualist discourses, for instance.

    The 'construct' character of Figure 2.1 thus clearly demonstrates the affinity between the phenomenological and structuralist approaches in its implicit critique of subject-centred reason.

[3]   Dialogical interaction necessitates a content or communicative act held in common which is hence the property of neither conversant/interactant. It must be emphasised that dialogical relations can be understood to cover both micro, interpersonal and macro, institutional situations. In the latter case dialogue encompasses one's interactions with adverts, fashion, broadcasts, architecture, the temporal structures of representations (see Chapter 7), and so on.

[4]   See Grimshaw (1996, p.22) for a criticism of the assumption that 'anything...historically, geographically or culturally remote could not be significant'; that it could not 'speak' to us.

[5]   Farrell (1995, p.27) argues that Davidson takes an Hegelian-style view that reason is imbricated in the world and Grayling (1985, Chapter 3) suggests that Davidson sees the senses as providing a semantic structure to the world. D'Amico (1989, p.130) claims that Davidson rejects the external-internal formulation of the knowledge-world relation. Given that Davidson is not a Rortian coherence theorist, there is still no indication of how semantic depth could work, as Davidson has rejected the meaningfulness of natural language.

[6]   See also Rorty (1991, 1993) and responses from Fraser (1989) and Wilson (1992).

[7]   Rorty's point that metaphors die and acquire literal meanings ignores Derrida's (*op. cit.*) claim that the wearing away of metaphor cannot erase its trace, or, in our terms, its irreducible indexicality. It also raises the suspicion that the gap between metaphorical and literal utterances is not the yawning chasm presented by Davidson.

    Worn-out metaphor is precisely the kind that interests phenomenology because its meanings are taken for granted in the literal statement. It operates, in Ricoeur's (1986, p.284) terms, 'behind our backs' and thus emphasises the decentered nature of discourse and subjectivity.

3   Intersubjectivity and Rationality

Two themes are central to this discussion of rationality. Firstly, that perceptions, judgments and theoretical generalisations are situated rather than absolute. Secondly, that all activity carries with it a substratum of unexamined, everyday constructs through which it 'makes sense'. In this chapter these insights are used to inform the discussion of rationalisation, agency, structure, institutional (bureaucratic) discourses, historical action, dialogical understanding, modernity, Enlightenment and 'other cultures'.

It is claimed that accounts of social life which ignore the intersubjective dimension inevitably both dichotomise and absolutise their subject matter; either the world is rendered all-powerful or its subjects appear as its absolute creators. In either case the origins of the shaping factor cannot be explained, as Rose (1981, pp.213-4) argues. Notions of unconditioned universal subjects such as the 'reasonable audience', ideal listener/communicator, and so on, will serve to illustrate the point.[1]

The life-world conception of the taken for granted, everyday features of life is taken as an initial example of this abstract way of thinking, in that it represents an at once arbitrary and absolute division of the social world where small-scale interaction, i.e. the realm of the subject, represents the domain of morality and freedom in contradistinction to the world of structural determination and unfreedom.[2] This has important consequences for the configuration of rationality in its dichotomisation of reason from spontaneity, objectivity from feeling, imagination or values from factuality, metaphorical from propositional language, theory from practice, representation from reality, common sense or popular ideologies from scientific discourse, and so on.

The Taken For Granted: Aspect or Domain of Meaning?

The life-world concept as employed by Husserl, Schutz (sometimes), Habermas and the current orthodoxy in sociology and cultural studies, functions for each in their own way to mark out a domain, a feature in an epistemological geography. Husserl's (1970) Galilean orientation drives him to locate ideal forms intuited from the everyday world in a separate, transcendental terrain. Schutz refers to transcendental life as that in which 'we-consciousness' operates, whilst Habermas cordons off the life-world from the social system and even separates it from the world of enlightened opinion, the area of *Diskurs*.

The view developed here is that the everyday is not in some sense a separate domain but rather the substratum of all activities. To take one example given by Schutz (1967, p.7): the 'thought objects of the social sciences [are] founded [upon] common sense constructs used...in everyday life'. Hence the world is experienced 'within a horizon of familiarity', that is, within taken for granted notions of what is 'typical' within existing experience: the world is apprehended via this 'natural attitude' (*ibid.*, pp.7-8).

Further, all activities occur in social contexts which give them their unique meaning or sense. The idea that meaning is wedded to context, or situated, although identified with Schutzian phenomenological social theory, is also found in Dummett's (1981) reading of Frege's work on meaning. Here it is argued that all cognitive, propositional type utterances depend for their specificity of meaning on the context of utterance. Dummett's point is that a context of unexamined notions is always present in natural language utterances. This equates in important respects with Schutz's conception of the way the natural attitude functions.

Garfinkel (1967, p.4) has elaborated this idea by arguing that utterances, however propositional, never completely eliminate the indexical aspect of communication - our descriptions of things always depend finally on a level of shared, so to speak, 'implicit' knowledge which situates the discussion, gives the meaning context and thus enables understanding to take place. Russell (1965b, p.336) argues that even where statements have no direct reference to specific contexts or experiences 'the problem of interpreting the descriptive phrases is exactly the same as if there were.' To put this another way, the use of such expressions implies situating conditions of the form 'what does this mean for me, here, now etc.'

Hence, in these texts the role of the everyday or intersubjective is crucial in picking out or identifying situations or other objects of discourse.

A further characteristic of the everyday order of language is that because it is essentially an activity, the epistemic and ontological divisions in thought undergo collapse. The notion of language as doing found here means that everyday identifications are 'done' rather than known, although their potentially explicable nature indicates that they are also the point of emergence of propositions about things.

On this view, the taken for granted, natural aspect of communication is *always* present in the use of abstract language; there is always a context to which it is applied, a situation within which it makes sense. This account of the everyday therefore departs radically from those of Husserl and Habermas in not compartmentalising the world in order to detect its rational features.

Having established the specificity of our account of the everyday, it is now possible to progress to examine in greater detail some of the problems with its 'topographical', that is, lifeworld-type readings.

Reason, Rationalisation and Common Sense

As Rose (1981, pp.1-13) notes, the social theory of Durkheim, Weber and, more recently, Habermas, has a neo-Kantian structure. It divides the social world into spheres of judgmental validity and values; a world of objective, value-free, instrumental reason and a world of ultimate goals proposed by free, (absolute) self-constituting egos (*ibid.*, p.214).

Hence, whilst the Aristotelian view of practical life entailed a coincidence between specific human activities and a sense of their ultimate worth, by contrast, in the time of modern capitalism, it is commonly argued, this connection has been critically eroded. This view is an element of a complex often referred to as the *Gemeinschaft-Gesellschaft* shift or contrast. In the work of Max Weber, but also that of Emile Durkheim, the development of a specialised division of labour leads to a separation between means and ends, an instrumentalism encroaching on everyday practices which is imposed on human subjectivity from outside as an 'iron law' of rationalisation.

In other words, Weber, Durkheim and Habermas have seen modernity in terms of a polarisation between rationalisation/increasing division of labour and a sphere of free human agency within which elements of *Gemeinschaft* can be preserved. These canonical writers formulate social life as an opposition between external determination by structures or systems and free interpersonal, small-scale, authentic interaction - with the consequent problem of how these spheres could possibly be related!

It is suggested that Schutz's view of the everyday offers a way out of this impasse in that it combines everyday accounts as practices with more structural features of the social world. The social world is something which is 'done' or achieved. For example, Schutz's approach to scientific rationality denies it an 'out-there' quality, rather it is something continuously in the process of constitution.

One way in which the rationalisation debate has become focussed is in relation to the instrumental reason-values dichotomy as found in the contrasting of science and common sense beliefs. Schutz's criticism of this demonstrates his concern with the practical, achieved quality of scientific knowledge. Now in social theory common sense is generally taken to embody a pre-scientific, pre-rational entwinement of values and practices. However, Schutz has argued that this Weberian ideal-type model of science cannot be found anywhere in reality. This is simply because science is not the rehearsal of already established knowledge where the experiment/theoretical account shows that an event of type A is governed by law B in such and such a way. Rather, it also involves judgements about new cases, that is, whether they fall under type A or not (Schutz, 1970b, p.109). At this point, the scientist's perspective, sense of relevance, mode of problematisation come into play (*op. cit.*, pp.108-9). These can shift periodically and lead to a new centre of interest as a consequence of the way science is recontextualised by its practitioners, where contextualisation is the taken for granted basis for paradigmatic concerns.

We can illustrate the idea of context by reference to Schutz's point about the application of types. Ideal types refer to particular schemes or fields of objects or areas problematisation which cover 'all the possible types to be used'. In other words, in applying ideal types we give an account of the instances to be considered as relevant to the application. The account entailed by application cannot itself be derived directly from descriptions of, or propositions containing, the types. It is only generated as an account or 'supplement' to the type through a 'principle of relevance', that is, by reference to *context* of application and its cultural assumptions about what is relevant to problematisation. For example, through the work of Althusser (1971) which developed the role of ideology in the production and reproduction of capital, feminists were able to point to the relevance of domestic labour to the reproduction of the social relations of production. In Schutzian terms, the 'subscripts' or cultural assumptions attached to housework had shifted allowing it to be considered as relevant to the reproduction of capital.

By means of Garfinkelian elaboration we can say that such an account exhibits an essential reflexivity in that domestic labour becomes part of the field of relevant types because of the practical issue, the shifting 'focus of interest' in the problematisation of social reproduction of capital. In other words, this is the way - given the shifting relation of cultural assumptions or types to a practice - theorists now wish to practise reproduction theory. The propositional and performative (application) features of science overlap at this point. The application of propositional knowledge to situations is, as Schutz (*loc. cit.*) notes, a way of determining its limits: 'The scientific problem [as a practice]...determines the limits within which possible propositions become relevant to the inquiry'. Thus phenomenology indicates the fundamental openness of so-called rationalised practices, institutions, etc. That is, their shifting everyday features tend to subvert the 'closure' and mystification/reification produced by the objectifying aspect of rationalisation (see Chapter 7 for further discussion of this).

Theories are hence not hermetically sealed conceptual structures 'out there' but always *situated*, that is, found in relation to practices where their concepts are linked in an horizon of typical familiarity to the cultural assumptions of their social practising. Schutz emphasises that this makes Weberian rationalisation manageable and enables the construction of social order. Hence:

> disenchantment [is]...the transformation of an uncontrollable and unintelligible world into an organisation we can understand and master, and in the framework of which prediction becomes possible...if social science has failed to consider this kind of rationalisation of its conceptual framework, each of us human beings, in 'just living along' has already performed this task, and this without planning to do so...we are guided neither by methodological considerations nor by any conceptual scheme of means-ends relations, nor by any idea of values we have to realise. Our practical interest alone, as it arises in a certain situation...and as it will be modified...is the only relevant principle in the building up of the perspective structure in which our social world appears to us in daily life (*op. cit.*, pp.96-7).

This view of rationalisation, unlike the more familiar Weberian conception of a world of pre-ordained ends and methods is also, as we have seen, the everyday world of scientific problematisation. The modern world looks considerably more negotiable through this perspective compared with the one encapsulated by the Weberian 'iron cage'.[3]

Schutz's reading of rationalisation has been criticised (O'Neill, 1995, p.182) on two grounds. Firstly, that for Schutz, 'scientific conduct is...ruled only by the norms of empirically adequate reasoning' and that this ignores the role of 'imagination', 'discovery', 'argument' and 'proof' which set off scientific from other kinds of activity. This is a misreading in the sense that Schutz acknowledges the need for a theoretical attitude and 'conceptual compatibility' but uses a postulate of empirical adequacy in the very specific sense of applying or giving an account of the theory. Here he is in the company of Popper (1972, pp.345-6), for example, who notes the use of rule of thumb methods in deciding whether a given case supports a theory.[4]

Secondly, O'Neill argues that in the case of social theory the application of norms of empirically adequate reasoning would indicate an intervention by instrumental rationality through the use of norms of everyday life in theoretical accounts of it. However, explicating the 'everyday' should here be understood as an account of the 'superscripts' or relevancies through which theories make sense in the context of application rather than a direct intervention by command institutions of state and economy. It signifies everydayness as the taken for granted of social science practice, which may be radically critical of affairs of state etc. This confusion evidently arises from O'Neill's use of the topographical view of the everyday where the latter is separated out from the sphere of enlightened opinion, *Diskurs*. Schutz is also inconsistent on this point. He refers, at one point (*op. cit.*, p.113), for example, to a contrast between daily life and culture. However, this does not detract from the plausibility of the non-topographical reading of 'everyday' as natural attitude.

O'Neill's stance effectively reproduces the dichotomy highlighted at the outset, between an inadequate subjective reason and the scientific or system problem as an 'out-there' beyond subjectivity. This is also a hallmark of the work of Habermas, to which we now turn.

Habermas, the Life-World and Resisting Rationalisation

Habermas (1987a, p.330) divides the social world into (micro) interaction and structure and places everyday life in the former. He argues that a domain of linguistic agreement/mutual understanding serves as a way of resisting the oppressive and distorting effects of rationalisation, *viz.* the imposition of reified means-ends relationships, relationships which are removed from value debates, that entail technical rather than substantive questions. However, the increasing colonisation of the lifeworld's common sense thinking by the symbolism of mediatised systemic imperatives

(Habermas, 1978b, p.196) leads him to suggest that undistorted communication and the salvation of the lifeworld is only possible from the sphere of *Diskurs*, that is, intellectual life. The structural/systemic world, by contrast, is the de-linguistified domain of money and power, a world beyond the horizon of interpersonal understanding (undistorted communication).

It is worth reiterating here that this is quite different from Schutz's 'everyday' which includes the world of work and administration. Outside the voluntary institutions where spontaneous interaction is possible and regulated by members' normative inclinations, the systemic sphere requires 'non-normative regulation of individual decisions that extends beyond the actors' consciousnesses' (Habermas, 1987b, p.117). Such systems regulate members' actions and self-interests by oppressive and distorting legitimations. Here 'steering media' of economic and state institutions 'stabilise the unintended interconnections of decisions that have not been subjectively co-ordinated' (*loc. cit.*).

Whilst this form of analysis is of interest in its own right, it also raises more general questions about the relationship between the everyday and subjectivity in the cluster of Weberian notions connoted by 'rationalisation'.

For Schutz, there is no impediment to extending action beyond individuals' consciousnesses nor indeed a problem with the decisions that have not been 'subjectively coordinated' and hence with 'unintended consequences'. Subjectivity has no intrinsic limitation to micro situations; 'unintended consequences' do not represent a *general* problem for social agents. As demonstrated above, Schutz believes that all these issues can be handled *intersubjectively*, in a mode where things are only 'occasionally propositional'. This is possible because of the accumulation of experience, 'stocks of knowledge', in short, the *biography* of the individual. The social world, however global its interconnections, is 'centred in the self of the person who lives and acts in it' (*op. cit.*, p.97).[5] That is, as Mead suggested, the social world is internal as well as external.

Therefore, as Gadamer (1981, p.495) argues on this more global sense of subjectivity, there is no reason why the world of labour should not be treated as interactive and not extra-linguistic. In fact, the world of work is 'the world of our power' - that we experience in mastering techniques of working', this is 'a way of research into ourselves'. Moreover,

> it is through and in the concrete experiences of our human existence, in domination and in work, and only here, that our human understanding of

ourselves...our conversation with ourselves, find their fulfilment and exercise their critical function.⁶

Further, the structures of state and economy work through social interactions. As Marx pointed out, capital is not just money or machinery; it is a social relation, not an abstract power. It works through relationships of production, buying and selling. Equally, the state, although an apparatus with a logic of its own, is at the same time a process of contested relationships. Although Habermasian delinguistified structures have logics, so do the everyday 'structures', working outside individual consciousness as a taken for granted substratum of conscious decision-making. Habermas's (1987b, p.338) positing of two logics - system and lifeworld - is arguably an excessive sociological compartmentalisation given that intersubjectivity contains aspects of both.

As we have suggested above, however rigid, formal, bureaucratic the codes of economic or state life may be, they have to be *interpreted* to be operationalised. This 'opening' indicates that the practising of codes relies on some supplement or account of how it should be done. In this way values, ideologies permeate the rationalised life, indicating what the code 'really means'.

The institutional analyses of Goffman, Strauss *et al.* show how bureaucratic rules and regimens are in fact *negotiated* via interpretation. Usually one remembers the code, though how it gets practised is less clear but no less important to the outcome. The idea of a 'negotiated order' (Strauss, 1968) depends then on the accounting procedures or interpretational actions of parties involved. The common sense logics of the situation are drawn upon to implement 'the rules'.

This raises a number of issues about Weberian rationalisation. Firstly, if rationalisation is, as a reality, a practised reality in the manner just described, then structure, as designated by formal codes, and interaction are coterminous. The dualistic characterisation of the social world is otiose. We can say that some structures are more central, powerful, dynamic than others, but that does not get round the point that they are *practised*. Secondly, the dualism of the Weberian perspective relies on a concept of action limited by the horizon of individual consciousness. Schutz and Mead, on the other hand, posit modes of we-relation and joint action through which group members create intersubjective structures, implicit or indexical ways of picking out realities which extend far beyond ideas that can be articulated propositionally. Thirdly, far from being concerned purely with technical mean-ends relations, the regulation of structures entails the structuring and practice of regulations through everyday, common sense notions.

Of course, for Habermas, the language of interpretation involves not only words but the capacities to distort and to dominate. However, as Wellmer (1985) has argued (Dews, 1987, pp.226-7), this does not quite grasp the way language functions in that official meanings are often supplemented by unofficial ones, as people interpret dominant articulations in their own situations. An example of this would be the way people 'read between the lines' of pronouncements in oppressive regimes. This is none the less a form of reading/communication. The ability of power to stifle communication is probably also somewhat overplayed with respect to sending messages. As Dummett (*op. cit.*, Chapters 6 and 19 *passim*) has argued, the 'context principle' enables indexical, metaphorical use (*oratio obliqua*) to convey meaning. This is not to deny that people are often misled by the information they are presented with. In these cases we would say that they do not grasp the *context*. For example, some messages divert attention from others which connote our subjectivities, 'speak to us' more fully in a broader communicative context. Here the preferred meanings encoded in communication practices obscure subordinate but more personally relevant readings. The notion of ideology as diversionary is appropriate here.

The use of types in the process of interpretation has been noted by Schutz (1967, p.3ff). However, here they generally function not to make knowledge claims but in the practical application of corrigible utterances to situations. Hence we can say that stereotypes, as exemplifying ideology, are an aspect of a practised oppressive reality rather than false statements about it. For instance, institutional racism works on the basis of applying types, hidden presuppositions about the size of ethnic minority families, desired areas of residence and so on. Here the types are seen as part and parcel of institutional practices rather than theoretical ideology/knowledge claims about ethnic minorities.

However, the Habermasian pessimism expressed in the notion of a lifeworld colonised by the dominant ideology can be seen as unwarranted for quite other reasons which are to do with the nature of social control. That is, there are many non-ideological factors contributing to domination which are ignored in Habermas's (1987a, p.330) equation of ideological colonisation of the lifeworld with social control in liberal democracies. Fear, insecurity, loss of morale and self-confidence, the sheer physical and mental exhaustion of daily life at the end of the twentieth century arguably all contribute to the engineering of consent. One is reminded here of

Dennis Wrong's (1961) view that social theorists can overplay the power of socialisation in getting people to do things.

It seems fair to conclude that Habermas underestimates the potentiality for resistance to rationalisation tendencies within the scope of the everyday, common sense or natural attitude (further discussed in Chapter 7), partly because of the restricted (lifeworld) notion of the everyday he uses, and that this will have implications of a mandarin sort. The focus on *Diskurs* as a space in which forms of domination can be contested suggests a 'leave it to the intellectuals' mode of practice.

Gramsci, Common Sense and the Articulation of Formal Discourses

Habermas's concern with a lifeworld micro-sphere of normative practice divorced from cognitive-instrumental knowledge finds an echo in Lockwood's view of rationalisation.

In his critique of Lockwood (1981), Benton (1984, pp.217-8) has examined the technicisation claims made about knowledge by rationalisation theory. He notes that Lockwood not only 'sees cognitive and normative...constraints on action [as]...analytically distinct' but also holds that they form 'the basis of a typology of action', that is, Lockwood sees people as actually differentiating their actions in this way. Benton counters this view with Gramsci's work on ideology and knowledge which recognises the inseparable interweaving of cognitive, sentimental and moral aspects of social action and that in contemporary circumstances these are not incompatible with theorising the system consequences of the rationality of capitalist class-actors.

It is important to understand the role of common sense in this 'inseparable interweaving'. For Gramsci (1971, p.377), the everyday accounting for, or appropriation of, bureaucratic-capitalistic goals or any other set of propositional-type claims, or programmatic sets of ideas occurs in cultural practices. Common sense is a substratum of such practices; it is the deposits of all previous knowledge; it is present as a sediment or 'trace' in linguistic practices; it is 'episodic' rather than logically consistent; it enables us to do things 'unconsciously', it can be enlivened, mobilised in ideologies; as such it 'create[s] the terrain on which men move, acquire consciousness of their position, struggle' (*loc. cit.*). Here common sense is intersubjective in Merleau-Ponty's sense of constituting understanding across contested positions and these encompass not merely the interpersonal but all the institutions of the 'integral state', that is, of society itself.

Educational practice illustrates Gramsci's (*op. cit.*, pp. 37 & 39) conception of intersubjectively-based understanding. He writes of the pupil with a traditional Italian curriculum that via Latin and Greek they are:

> plunged into history and acquired an historicising understanding of the world and life, which becomes a second - nearly spontaneous - nature...logical, artistic, psychological experience were gained unawares, without a continual self-consciousness...The end seemed disinterested because the real aim was the...formation of the personality by means of absorption and assimilation of the whole cultural past of modern European civilisation.
>
> [They learned Latin and Greek] in order to know at first hand...a civilisation that was a necessary precondition of our modern civilisation: in other words...in order to know themselves consciously. [Further,] it is the whole cultural tradition...which in a given ambience [teaching skilled at making the connections with contemporary life] produces such results.

Gramsci's point is that practically-oriented education makes conscious what is done anyway by reflex; that this knowledge is already part of us as we practice it daily. Education consists in bringing to the pupil's attention 'what they already know' so to speak. The cultural past is imbricated in language and these sediments can be articulated with the pupil's everyday experience. The passage also nicely delineates Gramsci's views on subjectivity: there are two aspects, the 'unconscious' (intersubjective) self and the conscious individual self, which exist in an interactive relationship.

In his analysis of ideology Gramsci (*op. cit.*, p.331) points to the way systems of ideas ('philosophies') can be articulated, via a political moment, with the common sense views of the people. This serves to mobilise common sense, and creates a terrain in which people come to recognise themselves and their social position (see Gramsci's observations cited above). Hence the account which ideology renders of common sense in their practical life, gives people not just ideational but *material* grounding, the institutional terrain of society is formed in this way. The term 'material' is apposite in that common-sense or practically-based ideologies exist beyond consciousness and shape it through the process of 'becoming aware'. Now the sense that people are caught up in and formed through practical ('organic') ideologies and their institutional terrains leads to the conclusion that linguistically, the objects or matters of our conversations connect us as conscious individuals to debates, understandings which we are historically predisposed to entertain through the connections between socio-cultural background and the tradition in which we are situated. There is an organic connection between personal biography and the wider cultural context. In a sense then we are formed by those debates themselves and our intersubjective understanding of them (see also the section on Gadamer below). At any particular point, the (linguistic) lines of argument could be said to be constitutive of subjectivity. Subjects are formed and receive their identities through the practices in which these debates are inscribed.

In contrast to Schutz, Gramsci (*op. cit.*, p.195) sees the construction of daily practice as *contested*. People draw on aspects of traditions which are congenial to their own situations, but the force fields of the contemporary issues and debates are decisive in shaping where the lines are drawn, how the sides line up ideologically, the 'differentiation and change in the relative weight of the elements' (cited in Mouffe, 1979, p.191). Gramsci's historicism clearly indicates that the cultural traditions are always available to us intersubjectively. In this, he goes against more recent claims (see Chapter 7) that cultural changes have made historical memory impossible. Such claims arguably mistakenly rest on the view that the sedimented culture does not continue to be articulated with current ideology, that is, enacted linguistically. Rather it must somehow be recuperated mechanically from education - be 'inculcated pedantically', in Gramsci's phrase.

Gramsci's work is poised strategically between the phenomenological and structuralist traditions and thus demonstrates the possibility of a productive conversation between them. These intellectual formations prompt their own - but none the less complementary- questions about the rationality of communicative activities.[7]

Quentin Skinner: Text as Action and Contestation

In view of what has been said about the absolutisation of agency as free consciousness and whether, alternatively, there is a sense to action which is not coincident with the agent's meanings, it is worth examining the debates around Skinner's (1988) account of historical action.

The exchanges between Skinner and his critics help to bring into relief issues about the rationality of historical agents and how we should view their beliefs. Skinner (*op. cit.*, pp.260-2) argues that the beliefs of historical agents should be seen not primarily as truth claims but rather as forms of action. Their utterances should be seen, following Austin (1980), as first and foremost, having an *illocutionary force*. That is, their meaning derives from what they do, what the writer intends to bring about by them, rather than from a *conventional or literal* grasp of their meaning. Hence, in assessing their rationality we must concern ourselves not with their overt epistemic implications but with how successful they are in expressing or bringing about a given state of affairs or event. Agents, Skinner (*op. cit.*, p.246) argues, may be deemed to be rational to the extent that they perform effectively according to the criteria of efficacy of a given time and place. The embracing of Protestantism by capitalists, for example, provided motivation by legitimation and must therefore be seen as rational to the extent that this enabled them to fulfil their pre-existing pecuniary goals (*ibid.*, p.113).

Skinner's use of the notion of legitimation suggests the operationalising of beliefs requires a use of language - an account of the beliefs - which persuades: 'X fits this outlook', 'Y is appropriate here', 'Z is illuminating', etc. This *metaphorical* use of language is also noted by Empson (1985, chapter 1, *passim*) and Heller (1984, p.162). It is a usage that reaches out to us, invites sympathy, is associative or connotes our own circumstances, invites action. To sum up this point: Skinner is arguing that even where language is couched in these ideological terms, when considered as successful action it is, none the less, rational.

Skinner (*loc. cit.*) builds on his idea of persuasive language to offer a picture not only of beliefs as action but as contestation. Different factions move history on by subverting existing meaning structures towards their own ideological programme and goals. Meanings are neutralised, inverted, extended, reduced and so on. Factions build on existing ideologies rather than starting from scratch (see also Gramsci, 1971, p.195) by contesting and rearranging elements of their meanings.

Taylor (1988, p.237) has, in criticism, raised the question of truth claims in relation to such beliefs; that there must be some relation between the efficacy of beliefs and their truth content. Through Dummett's work, we have posed this differently: what are the objective meanings (senses) expressed by such indexical (ideological) references? This is because we have argued that everyday beliefs work only indirectly or metaphorically rather than literally asserting that such and such a state of affairs pertains.

Taylor's point is important because it raises the matter of rationality in a wider sense than Skinner's behaviour-leading-to-satisfaction-of-intended-goals. That is, if 'contesting programmes of beliefs' is a viable description of historical action then the subject matter must have an underlying coherence which entails an ability to pose the question 'what is it that they are arguing about?'

Now Gramsci's (*op. cit.*, pp.330-31) work on ideology offers a formulation which includes these necessary elements via a notion of the contested articulation of sedimented common sense meanings to ideologies. That is, there is a political struggle over which articulation of common sense gives the best account of a formal ideological claim. Here 'common sense' is used in the non-topographical sense of the taken for granted basis of truth claims. 'Articulation' refers to the way abstract statements get operationalised and thereby become practical, convincing 'knowledge'.

How one decides which is the best articulation or appropriation of historical texts was, of course, for Gramsci and Skinner seen through the efficacy of 'text as action in context'. Barnes (1974) and Winch (cited *ibid.*, p.243), on the other hand, believe that as such a judgement requires one to stand on different ground, to be external to the context. It involves imposing other standards and leads to ethnocentrism. This issue is discussed below in relation to Gadamer's insights on dialogue and a fusion of horizons.

It can be seen from the discussion of Skinner and Gramsci that historical action and understanding are inescapably *political*. None the less, these processes are also conversational or dialogical. Moreover, whilst writers in the classical Marxist tradition of ideology have identified ideological processes as manipulative and distortional, Gramsci and Skinner have both emphasised their dependence on elements of rationality, that they make sense in terms of efficacy and existing cultural frameworks; also that they *limit* possible meanings in the sense that they rearrange ideologies, some ideas are displaced or become secondary to others from which they then derive their primary meanings.

Gramsci's account of ideology is fuller in the sense that he distinguishes the practical, 'organic' realm of ideology from the idealistic, programmatic dimension. This means that whatever actors' ostensible beliefs, their practical lives follow ideology-as-common-sense. Their 'collective' or intersubjective existence is the basis for the meaning of the account they give of political theory, that is, of formal party programmes. Hence the meanings that agents attribute to actions, contexts and so on, might be different from the sedimented logic or meaning of such 'texts' themselves. For Gramsci (*op. cit.*, p.324) the key problem of historical understanding is precisely 'knowing thyself', how the 'infinity of traces without an inventory' (cultural sediments) impinge on particular political contexts and identities. Therefore, unlike Skinner, Gramsci relies on a historicist notion of the common sense grounding of beliefs and cultural frameworks to make sense of actions and contexts.

For Gramsci (*op. cit.*, pp. 330-31) the success of one position in the contested dialogue involves its 'becoming popular', grasping the practical lives of a large enough constituency in such a way that those lives are positively addressed ('articulated') within the new programme and further, that alternative ways of addressing them have failed. On the other hand, Skinner's (*op. cit.*, pp.274-5) reliance on the pursuit of successful plans or programmes as a sufficient explanation of historical action follows Collingwood's model. For example, Collingwood reasons that because Nelson's plan for the Battle of Trafalgar was successful all we have to do to understand the situation is to grasp Nelson's strategy. However, 'Ideas', as Gramsci (*op. cit.* p.192) argues, 'are not "spontaneously" born in each individual brain: they have a centre of formation, of irradiation, of dissemination, of persuasion...'. They are 'structural and epistemological' rather than psychological (Gramsci, 1975, cited in Mouffe, *op. cit.*, p.191). This is to reiterate in a different way his point that the historico-cultural environment is something within which we act and, so to speak, 'live through', and whilst embodied in our discursive practices, it does not belong to any *individual* agent ('individuated consciousness'). Hence the problem for Skinner is that whilst the meaning of action is contextualised, this is never seen as a precondition which shapes agents' understandings but only as the way the agent brings things about. As Keane (1988, p.210) notes in his response to Skinner (1988): 'Interpreters [of actions] always already stand within this field of intersubjectively shared conventions and "preunderstandings"'. Therefore, understanding the effectivity or the rationality of action in context depends on recognising its intersubjective content as well as its meaning for individual agents and the extent to which the two coincide. In the case of the Battle of Trafalgar, this means we have to recognise that Nelson's victory was but one instantiation of a set of possibilities presented by the context of action. Further, this context is not reducible to what Nelson actually did. If it were, as with Collingwood, then Nelson's actions represent an absolutised subjectivity; it becomes impossible to ask why Nelson read the context the way he did, for Nelson's plans are taken as sufficient reason for what happened.

That is, it is not merely (as in Austin) that individual agents get language to do things, but that language is a medium which - as practised - generates its own collective meanings, common sense. Dummett (*op. cit.*, p.361) makes a similar point in relation to Davidson's claim that the meaning of utterances is conferred by their propositional content. For Dummett, this fails to distinguish between the *significance* (convention for indicating meaning) and the *sense* of the utterance, which he argues, exists independently of its conventional meaning. Utterances do things independently of whether we grasp them as doing so.

To summarise: using the philosophy of language we can say that dialogue works when both parties pick out the same states of affairs. The failure of 'conversations' in this respect may result in a shift in political allegiances. Hence, the success of ideologies depends on the practical, intersubjective skills of political actors. Grasping the logic of the situation however requires a *hermeneutics* of, for example, (as Gramsci points out), aspects of modern European history. It also signifies the historically determinate nature or limits to the linguistic meanings that agents can operate with. The absence of this frame of meaning in Skinner places him closer to Foucault's sense of historical contingency and irrationalism than Gramsci's historicism (Rosa, 1996, p.23).

On one important point Skinner and Gramsci are in agreement. This is that ideologies are not to be treated epistemically but rather as action in context. For Gramsci, this is because they are intersubjectively valid practical articulations of propositional language, that is, of programmatic ideologies. Consequently we can place his work on the functioning of ideas within the environs of a phenomenological philosophy of language.

Gadamer, Dialogical Understanding and the Problem of General Meanings

Gadamer (1981) follows the pattern of understanding via conversation or dialogue which we have seen in Skinner and Gramsci to the extent that there are two key interrelated issues raised by Gadamer which have a resonance with the other writers. These are 'how far is it possible to generalise one's own position' to which Skinner and Gramsci both answer in terms of the contestation of meaning and manipulation of language and secondly, 'from what cognitive position is criticism possible - universalism or overlap of perspectives'. Habermas (1980), who has figured prominently in the debates over Gadamer's hermeneutics, has argued in the style of positivistic philosophy of science that norms of discourse must be universally valid and, as such, approximate to an ideal speech situation.

Grimshaw (1996) has addressed this tendency in the work of Le Doeuff (1991), who whilst acknowledging the situatedness of the writer suggests that in the domain of philosophy, with its universalistic claims, the writer's audience should be universal. Now Grimshaw (*op. cit.*, p.22) agrees with the claim that, for example, feminists do not only speak to other feminists or those who share all aspects of the writer's social location, they may even appeal in totally unexpected ways as discourses always carry an excess of meaning beyond their conventional reception. However, Grimshaw (*op. cit.*, pp.24-5) argues, in an important sense Le Doeuff's conception of philosophical universalism is not 'universal' enough. Its use of the regulative idea of an appeal to the 'abstractly reasonable listener' does not recognise the Western and masculinist voice of much philosophical discourse. Grimshaw's (*op. cit.*, p.22) dialogical alternative to the abstract listener suggests that there are points at which our experiences overlap - as seen most clearly by the suggestion that we occupy multiple interconnected social locations which promote questions of common human concern (gender issues themselves provide an example). Hence dialogue is to be achieved by seeking out those points at which the traditions or perspectives concerned intermingle, 'speak to one', or, in Gadamer's (*op. cit.*, pp.272-3, 337) parlance, the points at which both parties are seeking answers to the same questions. For example, socialism and feminism can be seen as meeting in the context where patriarchal familial relations are argued to maintain production relations. As noted in Chapter 2, Gadamer describes such points as 'a fusion of horizons'.[8]

Using this notion, Grimshaw (*op. cit.*, pp.25-6) argues that feminists and others cannot and should not eschew the position from which they speak as the successful conversation preserves the particular perspective within the general. Hence, for feminist perspectivalism, this does not inevitably issue in a hermetic particularism of non-communicating monadic constituencies, but under the right circumstances - as exemplified above - produces, we can argue, something akin to the Gramscian process of articulation described above - the taken for granted features of a situation enable both parties to communicate through it and broaden their respective collective experiences whilst acknowledging the validity of their differences. The advantage of this view is that it avoids the pitfalls of abstract universals in the Hegelian style, where one position must win out in an absolute negation and supersession of the other's cognitive reach.

On the other hand, there are difficulties arising from Gadamer's own characterisation of situatedness. For Gadamer, the dialogical character of speech is founded on the cultural and intellectual tradition within which the speaker resides. Whilst, therefore, this provides a framework within which communication can take place, and hence avoids relativism in that it fixes the terms of the exchange between speakers, it is none the less still vulnerable to a charge of irrationalism - an absolutism of the structures of tradition - on the grounds that the tradition of a speaker might not be relevant to the issues and context in which they attempt to engender understanding. Gadamer has dealt with this objection, as noted in Chapter 2, by declaring the possibility of openness to meanings which go against the tradition as it stands. However, if this is so, then it is difficult to see how one is situated rather than free-floating with regard to intellectual influences. How can one be capable of seeing the truth of ideas extraneous to one's own tradition? Warnke (1987, p.106) notes that Gadamer fails to distinguish clearly two senses in which speakers or positions might be in agreement. The tradition is firstly 'an integral part of our own self-understanding', we share its cultural assumptions whether we support its more programmatic aspects or not; secondly, we may undergo a 'critical and reflective integration' into it. Gadamer's elision of tradition as a condition of understanding with the more conservative position through which, as Warnke (*loc. cit.*) notes ' we are not only members of a tradition but also its ideological supporters' fails to recognise this distinction. The reaction of Habermas (1977) to this irrationalism is, however, as shown above, only capable of reinstating the individual as a unified unsituated consciousness, and hence, offers no solution to the question of how we can understand each other and yet disagree. As was suggested in the section on Skinner and Gramsci, the more plausible scenario, (also argued strongly by Merleau-Ponty, 1962, p.362, following Hegel) is that dialogue depends on a measure of disagreement; speakers contest and modify each other's positions. Albrecht Wellmer (1986), writing in the tradition of critical theory, has also rejected the link between consensus and communication, favouring instead a constitutive plurality of signusers and identifying the idea of an ideal (consensual) communication community with stasis and 'a cancellation of the linguistic-historical life-form of human beings' (cited in Dews, *op. cit.*, p.323).

Whilst Gadamer appears to confuse the prejudice/common sense and critical reflection aspects of communication in his discussion of a fusion of horizons, Dummett (1981) arguably presents a way out of this difficulty. The comparable distinction in Dummett is between natural language utterances, their taken for granted meanings, and the senses which statements in such language come to express and which can react back on speakers' usage and their grasp of the state of affairs discussed. Senses are expressed through the application of intersubjectively held truth conditions (which cannot be exhaustively specified) to statements. X can see what Y is getting at even where they disagree about how the truth conditions should be applied, that is, whether a particular case is relevant to the type of situation under discussion. Hence, intersubjective reflection and agreement are separate features of communication practices. Within Dummett's (*op. cit.*, p.134) reading of Frege speakers' meanings are not consensually fixed, rather the senses of communicative practices are open to different readings and in shifting contexts can generate new propositions as existing ones take on the role of the everyday or taken for granted, that is, become background or context for new thoughts (see Chapter 5).

Gadamer (*op. cit.*, pp.333-5) is well aware of the distinction between agents' meanings and the logic of a situation, as is clear from his criticism of the Collingwood (and, *a fortiori*, Skinner) view of meaning. In effect, however, he does not allow for theoretical meanings, explicit self-understanding as opposed to taken for granted meanings of the tradition. Language is a store of meaning, a means of expressing truths rather than identifying them. Dummett's (*op. cit.*, pp.162-3) position, on the other hand, suggests that a process of identification is always at work within communication: speakers pick things out, even if only indexically (where identification is deferred from one utterance or expression to others within that communicative context).[9] This enables us to talk intelligibly about, for example, the nature of a tradition *even though our meanings remain incomplete*. By contrast, Gadamer's conflation of situatedness and self-understanding leaves the question of identifying the limits of a tradition unanswered. Tradition is absolutised and historical agents fixed within it.

Some Consequences of Dialogical Method

One of the merits of the preceding discussion for social theory is that it enables us to recast the problem of ideology in primarily ontological terms. Ideology is seen variously in terms of natural language utterances, acts, practices rather than clear cognitive assertions although the latter are reflected in these doings. As Gadamer (1977, p.38) notes, the intellectual impact of the tradition 'is inevitably more being (*Sein*) than consciousness (*Bewusstsein*)', it is 'effective history'. Hence beliefs should not be sociologically assessed in the language of distortion and reflection but rather as evidence of changes in the composition of society. If such changes lead to heightened contradictions, as did, arguably, those during the Thatcher-Reagan period, then the solution to those conflicts lies not in critiquing market economics in an abstract way but in examining the effects of its practical applications, its situated realities. As Gadamer (1982, pp.338-9) points out, the intellectual habit (stemming from Kantianism) of regarding problems in the abstract, that is, as having one for-all-time formulation disregards their continual historical reconstitution. Gramsci makes an in some ways similar point when he observes that the hegemonic powers in new historical conjunctures produce a rearticulation of key problems, they reassemble the ideological inventory to suit their own practical needs. The 1980s move towards addressing economic issues in monetarist rather than Keynesian terms illustrates this insight. None of this precludes rational judgement and this is given illustration in Gramsci (*op. cit.*, p.333) when he claims that the worker's situated, organic or 'spontaneous' and practical consciousness represents reality and often contradicts the programmatic formulations of the professional ideologists.

The theme of ideology as dialogical practice which has ontological implications can be related to Gadamer's (*op. cit.*, p. 341) elaboration of conversation as a situating, transformative process. The linguistically positioned object of a conversation 'is not a possession at the disposal of one or other of the interlocutors' rather the conversation and its object 'presupposes...or creates a common language'. Further, the conversants do not 'adapt themselves to one another, but rather, in the successful conversation they both come under the influence of the truth of the object and are thus bound into a new community.' And, contra Rorty's idea of self-development, the eventuation of

> an understanding...in a dialogue is not merely a matter of total self-expression and the successful assertion of one's own point of view, but a transformation into a communion, in which we do not remain what we were.

The transformative, open character of dialogue is also emphasised by Gadamer (*op. cit.*, pp.388-9) in his critique of Enlightenment methodology. He argues that the Enlightenment approach to problems is to see them as entirely subsumed under trans-historical typologies. System concepts are seen as 'generic' rather than modifiable by changed historical circumstances - this includes references by the Enlightenment to its own validity (*ibid.*, p.239ff). This criticism has a very real relevance to 'enlightened opinion' today in that commentators on the world situation refer to issues precisely in such terms: 'the West', 'the former Soviet Union', Islamicism, feminism, the 'industrialised world' and so on.

The reifying influence of the cover concepts makes it difficult to think beyond them. However, the significance in doing so is perhaps decisive for the plausibility of Gadamer's notion of tradition. In reality there are no traditions in the hermetic sense. Historical movements of population with their linguistic influences, the colonial period, industrialisation, globalised trade and media - even international conflict - produce understanding in the sense outlined above and in doing so help to explode the myth of localised limits to effective communication.

The fusion of horizons can accommodate 'outside' influences because in some sense they are already there, inside. Hence, it is not a question of attempting to understand something completely different. It is perhaps also worth mentioning here Davidson's (1986) comment (cited in Farrell, 1994, pp.174-80) that in entertaining the idea of 'the other' we are already characterising an entity as a part of our own rational world, which is, consequently, for Davidson *the* rational world. Hence the (confused) logic in the posing of the 'rationality and other cultures' question - it has already delineated what otherness is; it is familiar with what it does not know!

In the context of such considerations providing the grounds for a fusion of horizons, MacIntyre (1985), as Warnke (*op. cit.*, p.172) notes, has addressed the conditions under which explicit borrowings from other traditions are made. MacIntyre argues that a fusion occurs when a tradition has a problem that it cannot solve in its own intellectual terms. Hence, again, it is presupposed that canons of rationality are shared with other traditions and are, arguably, in Davidson's terms, features of the world, real but also discursive properties.

Rationality, Modernity and Situatedness

Grimshaw's (*op. cit.*, p.26) comments on the significance of a fusion of horizons for an understanding of the growth of knowledge point to cognitive perspectivalism and a deabsolutised conception of intellectual progress. The inference here is to the problematic nature of an Hegelian conception of knowledge in which substantial progress transcends existing intellectual achievement and frameworks to the extent of denying them any independent validity. By contrast, a fusion of horizons preserves and broadens existing insights, in this way it is in Warnke's (*op. cit.*, p.165) view a form of 'deabsolutised' negation.

Now the importance of this point should not be lost in investigating intellectual and cultural formations of modernity. One way of putting this is to address Western modernity in terms of its others - the formations that are a part of Western development and yet denied recognition as such. Third World nationalisms, the phenomenon of underdevelopment, 'world music', exemplify this point.

Within European social thought itself 'other' conceptions of the world including socialism, feminism, ecologisms, literary Romanticism, communitarianism, fascism, national and familial ideologies and discourses clearly figure, but only as a kind of backdrop, a taken for granted although alternative, contesting framework for 'modern' modernity. There is therefore a *counter-modernity* which grounds or situates the talked about, dominant themes of Western values, rationalised markets and production, technicised objectives and so on.

Further, whilst the debates about community (*Gemeinschaft*) and association (*Gesellschaft*) in social theory are conducted not only as if *Gemeinschaft* were only proper to the traditional world and exists now only as a residue but also take social science to have superseded the *Gemeinschaft* organicist worldview, this ignores the fact that the theorists themselves employ the *Gemeinschaft* framework as a means of validating modernity! As Nisbet (1972, p.17) observes, sociology is heavily indebted to this premodern perspective in 'concept', 'symbol' and 'attitude'. There were 'deep currents of conservatism' in the work of Simmel, Weber and Durkheim.

There is, none the less, a tendency to equate intellectual modernity with the Enlightenment. Consequently, sociology has fallen into the Enlightenment trap of thinking that because it is modern it is historically unconditioned and unaffected by *Gemeinschaft* culture, that the latter's concepts have no constitutive role for modernity and that, by implication, sociological debates are not situated.

This neo-Kantian aspect of the Enlightenment has been criticised (Rose 1981, pp.211-14) in the sociological methodology of Weber and Durkheim. In the one case society is an absolute foundation for the individual (Durkheim) and vice versa in the other. There is no conception of mediating transformative practice or situating and situated subjectivity and hence the individual and society appear as absolute opposites rather than products of historically-situated activity.

The 'abstract' or 'generic' tendency at work here to equate the thought of modernity with the Enlightenment is also fundamental to postmodernist critiques of the modern, for example, Lyotard (1984). The irony of using Enlightenment methods against the Enlightenment should not escape us here!

Gadamer's (*op. cit.*, p.194) observation that the 16th and 17th centuries contained a nominalist tendency later culminating in Kantianism supports this view of the Enlightenment. However, Farrell's (*op. cit.*, pp.16-17) comment that Hegel saw reason as embodied in nature together with Marx's realism (Keat and Urry, 1975, Chapter 5) and tendency to denounce abstract thinking, in, for example, his 'Theses on Feuerbach', suggest a different angle. This is that although nominalism, conventionalism, or in Adorno's parlance, 'identity thinking' were perhaps the cultural dominant of the Enlightenment, reflecting the instrumentalist orientation of capitalism and its administration, Illuminism was nevertheless a *contested* tradition.

Notes

[1]   See Rose (1981, pp.33-6, 213-4) for an account of this in the social theory of Durkheim, Weber and Habermas.

[2]   Globalisation theory marks a welcome shift away from this. See Hall in Rutherford (ed.) (1990) on diasporic identities, for example.

[3]   The sociological canon, however, tends to stress only the objectifying side of rationalisation. Whilst it is true that Schutz sees the achievement of social order as a relatively unproblematic consensual procedure, as Heller (1984, xi-xii) notes, and has no critique of ideology/fetishised social relations and the inverted character of representation under commodified social life, his notion of the open horizon of typicalities provides a powerful way of understanding how social objectifications are undermined in practice.

[4]   See Chapter 2 for McDowell's (1994) point that agreement about conceptual content and meanings is always in the end a matter of ostensive definition: the situatedness of meaning always renders one's position open to further explanation *viz.* 'this is what I mean'.

D'Amico's (1989, p.131) suggestion that for Popper the 'human senses are theoretical hypotheses about the world' is interesting in that respect as is Popper's (*loc. cit.*) own comment about relevance being determined by a 'horizon of expectations'.

[5]   See Wagner (1973) and Smart (1976) for similar readings of Schutz and the discussion of macro situations by Schutz in Chapter 2 of the current work.

[6]   For Gadamer (*op. cit.*, pp.159-66, 330), the basic element of conversation is not interpersonal interaction but the relation of a questioning subject to a text - whether this be direct speech, written text or by extension of this argument, the mass media - which would also be understood by reconstruction or articulation in the context of its reading.

7   On the affinities between structuralism and phenomenology see, for example, Silverman (1987).

8   Arguably here the result is a new theoretical object rather than merely a contradiction between pre-existing accounts of socialism and feminism. Grimshaw (*op. cit.*, pp.21-2) makes a similar point about how feminism and philosophy reconstitute each other as 'feminist philosophy' rather than 'feminism *plus* philosophy'.

9   Even in indexical communication conceptual identities play a part. The point for Dummett (*loc. cit.*) though is that such identities are not self-sufficient but always situationally related and therefore the meanings of natural language expressions remain incomplete (open-ended). The communicative content of natural language is not amenable to conventional reading/closure. See also McDowell in Note 4 above on the permeability of concepts to situational meaning.

4　From Structuralism to Phenomenology: Connotation, Denotation and Meaning Context

We turn here to examine semiotic and context perspectives of meaning in the light of the question of how it is that coherence is achieved in systems of signs, even where they are, as in ideologies, clearly contradictory. The connotative power of metaphorical language is seen as a key factor in integrating signs into discourse and also in understanding the materiality or real-world dimension of language.

Connotation and the Coherence of Discourse: The Legacy of Althusser

The coming-to-be of metaphor, Beardsley (1958, pp.138-47) has argued, depends on the outweighing of the sense of overwhelming contradictoriness in contrasted terms by the meaningfulness of such contradictoriness. A key element of this is the sense of cohesion between the terms in question. This section looks at the way such a cohesion factor is handled in the structuralist tradition of social theory.

Althusser, and following him, Laclau, offer a theory of the unity of ideological formations; that is, they give an account of how it is that various ideological elements cohere to produce a belief system. Central to this theory is the idea that different bits or elements of a belief system cohere because they have an affinity for each other; they connote one another. Following the line of argument taken in this book this is important because symbolic systems are a moment of social reality, inseparable from the social practices they represent, and indeed, which they express. Hence, to understand the coherence of symbols is also to grasp the unity of social practices in any given milieu. As Hall (1986a) argues, the more general the congruence or harmony between the symbolic elements of a social formation, the stronger is the system itself. Where, however, the connoting power rests on a central symbol almost entirely, it is clear that alternative connotations constantly threaten to undermine this symbolic predominance. In other words, in such cases, the connotative force that holds between the elements of the system is not akin to that which holds between the central symbolic element and the rest. Hall (*loc. cit.*) cites Thatcherism as an example of this. Because of the lack of connotative cohesion between its non-central elements, Hall argues that Thatcherism is a highly contested ideology.

In the Althusserian paradigm, effective ideological discourses manage to displace and neutralise the contradictory images which are present in their elements, but this suppression of alternative meanings is always provisional and dependent on specific historical circumstances.

Central to Hall's analysis of the discourses of Thatcherism is Althusser's use of the language of psychoanalysis to convey the contradictory nature of social processes. Laclau and Mouffe (1989, pp.97-98) point out that although psychoanalysis uses a language of the symbolic, in Althusser this does not denote a separate concern with the examination of discursive features of the social but is rather a novel way of talking about social relations and structures themselves. Indeed, for Althusser, it is argued, 'the social constitutes itself as a symbolic order'. This is exemplified in the process of condensation where a number of images/relations are compressed into one. Closely related to this is the notion of overdetermination where one image/relation is privileged as that into which others are condensed, or displaced. Displacement and condensation are complementary processes, that is, condensations generally function to displace contradictions. The operation of displacement involves the transference of psychic energy from one image to another. In Althusser displacement functions to neutralise social contradictions by shifting the attention from one image/relation to another; this displaces the contradictions emerging in the subjectivity (identity) of individuals. Althusser (1977, p.206, f.46) says of the notion of overdetermination: 'it is borrowed from two existing disciplines: specifically from linguistics and psychoanalysis' whose character is sufficiently dialectical to make the relationship between form and social content 'not...an arbitrary one'.

Further, Laclau (1987, p.93), in analysing the cohesion of ideological formations, cites Laplanche and Pontalis (1967) on the Freudian notion of condensation as showing it to have both psychological and linguistic relations. In dream imagery:

> A single representation represents...many associative chains at the intersection of which it is situated...it is then invested with energies which, attached to those different chains, add to it...

Moreover, condensation is not like 'a resume', condensed symbols are not like concepts, which have a definite ordering and ranking of their contents, rather symbols can draw on or accentuate any of the different latent meanings (connotations) which are present in all of the manifest meanings.

If this Freudian-linguistic model is translated, as with Althusser and Laclau, into the realm of ideology as it impinges on the individual subject then we can talk of systems of symbolic representations becoming articulated with an individual's own symbolic inventory. Laclau (1987, p.100ff), following Althusser (1971) describes this as a process of *interpellation* of the individual within an ideological discourse. This means that the individuals come to recognise themselves within the discursive resources conveyed by the ideology. Such a discursive identification of the individual entails, following the account of condensation above, a relation to the ideology which accentuates the sense of subjectivity already present in the individual's symbolic resources. The chains of symbolic associations present in the ideology will connote or condense already existing images of self.

Laclau (*op. cit.*, p.102) further elaborates this notion: 'Different types of interpellations (political, religious, familial, etc.) [can] coexist whilst being articulated within an ideological discourse in a relative unity'. This is not a *logical* ordering of ideas, but rather a *connotative* unity of ideological elements. For example, if a wife and mother (familial element) is a good housekeeper/consumer (connotes economic life), a 'working mother' (connotes a work relation) and a family member who votes with her husband (connotes politics) then the familial element is overdetermined by a cluster of other elements which thereby render it more meaningful, that is, connect it to a reinforcing system of ideas.

When social systems succeed in conferring such identities on their individual subjects, the contradictions implicit in these identities are said to have been displaced or neutralised. In this way the assumptions behind the ideology remain taken for granted knowledge. An example of displacement would be the associative chain of connotations around the idea 'freedom'. 'Freedom-equality-liberty-licence-everyone for themselves' is a possible associative chain here. Some of the elements get displaced in the free market ideology of liberalism - 'licence' and 'everyone for themselves', for example. It could be argued that they are consequent upon the practice of the other elements, and contradict the notion of liberty, but that such a contradiction gets displaced in the practice of the ideology. This means that as the ideology creates identities for individuals, the elements of individuals' self-conceptions which get overdetermined will rearticulate those which echo the anarchic-egoistic elements so that they lose their contradictory character. In this way, for Laclau, the ideological moment of social practices involves the recombination and displacement of their elements.

Althusser, Spinoza and the Discursivity of the Real

The Laclau-Althusser formulations of the relationship between symbolic and social processes suggests the productivity of a Spinozist reading of Althusser. The Spinozism of Althusser (Collier, 1991, p.89) needs to be spelled out if the theoretically revolutionary import of the notion of overdetermination for a discursive account of the real is to be appreciated.

Spinoza departs radically from the various forms of mind-body dualism prevalent in the ideas of modernity. Firstly, for Spinoza, ideas are equally material with the spatial-physical aspects of the world. Secondly, the relationship between individual parts and the whole of a system is such that the whole is expressed in the individual parts. Hence, the whole can be affected by itself, non-paradoxically, as expressed ('displaced') in the parts.

The radicalism of this approach in its bearing on the symbolic is captured appropriately in the linguistic trope of metaphor. Metaphor (see below) embodies both the 'condensation' or part - whole function of language, and also through the notion that the usage of metaphorical language *does* something - brings about a state of affairs that it expresses. This is reminiscent of Garfinkel's (*op. cit.*, p.4) statement that natural language has a duality of functions, it both describes and in describing organises a state of affairs. It is language as action.

To grasp the idea that the symbolic and the real are inextricably intertwined, it is worth returning to Laclau's (1979, pp.97-8) account of Althusser (1971): the symbolic aspects of overdetermination are not to be seen as secondary: 'there are not two planes, one of essences and the other of appearances'. The social is not a primary, literal level which fixes the meanings of the symbols in ideology; there can be no such *a priori* relationship between symbols and social structures. Social relations just are, at one and the same time (overdetermined) symbols *and* structures.

(One can agree with this account without following Laclau's leap in considering that because the literal is non-primary this effects its complete abolition - see below for discussion of the role of 'the literal' as linguistic codifers/formulae.)

Now, from a Spinozist perspective, the elision of symbols and structures can be expressed as follows. Crucially for Spinoza, the mind is the idea of the body. This can be interpreted as meaning simply that ideas and brain processes are identical. However, as Collier (*op. cit.*, pp.77-9) argues, a more plausible interpretation is that whilst there is an identity between the ideational and spatially extended human spheres, there is also an implication that an individual's bodily relationship with its environment is mirrored in the configured complexity of its ideas. The configured complexity of the ideas varies according to the concomitant complexity of the body's relations with its environment. Now, whilst Spinoza considered only the relationship between a body and its physical environment, Collier (*op. cit.*, pp.82-3) argues that there is no good reason for not extending the theory to cover other human beings as well. On Collier's extended version, the spatial configuration of an individual's relation to others also exists under the ideational/symbolic attribute. Hence ideas/symbols have an objective, material import. They are not subjective entities, but exist independently of their appropriation by particular individuals.

In the same way, we can consider ideology in Althusser as a material entity. An important aspect of the materiality of complex bodies (e.g. society) or ideas (e.g. ideology) is the way they cohere. For Spinoza (Collier, *op. cit.*, p75) there is a binding force or *conatus* which accounts for their continued existence. We can straight away see from this that there is a non-arbitrary relationship between Spinozism and the linguistic-psychoanalytic apparatus in Althusser.

If we follow through the notion of coherence-as-connotation in Althusser and Laclau, then connotation is the force through which ideological formations and their conferral of subjectivities (identities) continue to exist. As Althusser (1971, p.160) observes in the 'paradoxical' style we noted above, 'The category of the subject is constitutive of all ideology', but only 'insofar as all ideology has the function [which defines it] of "constituting" concrete individuals as subjects'. Hence concrete individuals are the condition of possibility of ideology because it takes a configuration of individuals to provide the notion of a subject; a matrix of partial interpellations which can then feed back into those individuals in ways which connote their specific characteristics, that is, constitute them as *particular* socially overdetermined subjects (see Laclau above on interpellation).

A similar reciprocation would be apparent if we were to look at the way individual structures within a social formation were overdetermined, that is, in terms of the processes of condensation and displacement which facilitated the coherence of the formation. For example, the structure in dominance (capitalist mode of production) appears as a particular aspect of the formation but at the same time it is constituted out of the interconnections between all the institutions, and as such is the structure of structures. In another case, whilst ideologies are one of the conditions of the reproduction of capitalist social relations, they are also taken as aspects of the relations of production, the way they are lived.

The foregoing formulation of overdetermination has interesting consequences for realism in that there is no hidden essence determining *a priori* the relations, structures of social formations (Keat and Urry, 1975, p.135).[1] A similar comment applies to the use of overdetermination in language as it appears in the structure of metaphor (see discussion of Ricoeur below).

Ideology as Lived Experience

The similarities between structuralism and phenomenology should not be underestimated. The Althusserian notion of discursive practice has its echo in Garfinkel's action (as agents giving an account) that is also a description or Dummett's natural language utterances. Indeed, Althusser's claim that theoretical practice is itself a party to the world has its counterpart in Dummett's claim that speakers' utterances express a reality in successful communication (the sense of the utterance).

Althusser notes that a particularly significant feature of ideology is that its (interpellated) subjects experience themselves as concrete, free beings outside ideological determination. In phenomenology, the experience of the everyday is the common sense, *taken for granted* understanding of the world in which agents do not consciously consider their situatedness. Further, whilst Schutz (1974, p.104ff) distinguishes the taken for granted as typical construct or thought object of common-sense understanding from ordinary consciousness, Althusser (1977, p.233) notes of ideology:

[it] is indeed a system of representations, but in the majority of cases these representations have nothing to do with 'consciousness': they are usually images and occasionally concepts, but it is above all as structures that they impose themselves on the vast majority.

In *Lenin and Philosophy*, the Gramscian legacy is apparent in Althusser's siting of ideology in everyday institutional practices and rituals, a further accentuation of its pre-given, natural, obvious, everyday character.

However, it should be clear that Althusser does not offer a theorisation of the everyday as a necessary component of discursive practices in the manner in which Garfinkel, Dummett or Russell (see below) identify the inevitable natural language base or indexicality of all propositional (theoretical, for example) utterances.

Althusser does offer a theory of the subject, but this is based in Lacan's psychoanalytic notion that the subjectification process is grounded in transcendental archetypes of, for example, the mother or father and that whilst the unconscious is a symbolic order, the symbols 'the name of the father', and so on, are not intersubjectively generated, as Dews (1987, pp.240-1) notes, but come from an eternal symbolic inventory beyond the screen of the unconscious.

Now, whilst Althusser bases the crucial concept of overdetermination in the psychoanalytic and linguistic traditions of structuralism, we will pursue it through the idea of connotation and the structure of metaphor. Connotation will be examined both within the structuralist/semiotic and semantic/dialogic traditions and an attempt will be made to discover its relation to these. We will query whether it is completely tied to structuralism or if there is a phenomenological contribution to its operation.

Semiotic Theories of Meaning and the Context Issue

Current theories of meaning are heavily influenced by structuralist (Saussure, Barthes) and poststructuralist (Derrida, Foucault) ideas. One of the key ideas from the work of Saussure (1966) is that terms themselves are not the bearers of meaning. Rather, it is the difference between two terms that generates meaning. In other words, terms are related by their difference. Difference seems to precede or structure terms themselves. It becomes a metaphysical principle.

Whilst it is a truism to say that every term is different from every other term, there is a sense in which some differences do not really matter.

For example, in common usage the difference between 'elephant' and 'rhubarb' or 'drawing pin' seems arbitrary and meaningless. In other words, in the Saussurian sense of difference not all differences seem to count; they are not all meaningful. Saussure argues that this is so because of the nature of the relations between terms. That is, differences between terms take *paradigmatic* or *syntagmatic* forms: they exclude relation or exhibit combinatory potential respectively. This formal demarcation does not of itself get us any closer to understanding why it is in a particular circumstance that terms do or do not combine, etc. Consequently, it can be argued against Saussure that difference on its own is not sufficient to account for the production of meaning; that the merely arbitrary deployment of the difference principle - for this is what it must be without other guiding principles - cannot guarantee the production of meaning.

It can be argued that meaningful differences are ones where the terms to be differentiated also have some association. For example, 'left' and 'right' are different but also relational in the sense that they have an extra discursive reference, that is, they occur in a common context. Hence it can be further argued that these terms have an element of resemblance as well as difference because they both connote the same type of context - that of spatial location. They both summon up the same kinds of issues, those concerning orientation in space. Differentiation is therefore, it would seem, dependent upon that which is being distinguished having a resembling or relationally unifying quality with its contrast.

The fact that meaning seems to be produced within a complex of resemblance and difference suggests that these functions exist in an irreducible unity; that each term owes a debt to that which it is differentiated from and can therefore never be fully differentiated or semantically independent from it. In structuralism this means, in effect, that the process of naming - which seeks to suppress context by paradigmatically excluding other names in order to classify its syntagma requires complementation by a moment of 'naming-in-context' if the reality of what is named is to be preserved in the meaning generated. Further, if the names which are excluded or displaced are brought back then no extra meaning is obtained in this semiotic framework as the meaning of a term is its difference from what it excluded. 'Difference theories' of the structuralist and poststructuralist type suggest such a reductive view of meaning because they elevate differentiation or the substitution of names into a first principle and contextual resembling meanings such as those given by the discursive context of an utterance add nothing.

The argument that differences always occur in contexts and that the key to understanding meaning is to be found in a context-based view of connotation and metaphor, will be taken up again later in the chapter.

From Connotation to Sedimented Meaning: Laclau, Jameson, Schutz

The suggestion made above that meanings relate to contexts of utterance, that they must have a quality of 'aboutness' as well as relating to other meanings, leads us into an examination of a second key notion of Saussurian theory. This is that it follows from the rejection of the idea that terms are bearers of meaning that objects themselves are also bereft of any intrinsic meaning. Taking an object (in the symbolic sense) as a term, then its meaning is generated by its juxtaposition to another object/term. The gap between the signifier, the tangible representation of meaning and the unit of meaning itself, the signified, can never be closed; neither can their relationality be theorised. Signification is arbitrary with respect to its meaning content.

Signifiers and signifieds form lateral series both of which have their own logic and therefore there are limits to what can be effectively represented by any particular semiotic structure, in that it must have a logic which parallels that of the meaning structure. This argument is made well enough by Levi-Strauss (1964, p.89) in his work on the Nuer where he observes that the Nuer use the symbolism of birds to explain inter-familial relations because it is 'good to think with'. That is to say the symbolism has a parallel logic to familial relations; it makes the distinctions required for the grasping of family structure.

However, in poststructural theories, semiotic structures are infinitely plastic with regard to meaning. There are no limits to the semantic repertoire produced by the play of difference because semiotics posits no internal (sedimented) and specific relationship between terms and meanings. A given representation (symbol) can represent anything. Poststructural theories of ideology, for example, Laclau (1987, p.111) suggests that the terms of say, fascist ideologies, could be used as a grid for proletarian identity, and hence that the subjectivity of the working class as represented in popular ideologies could be made amenable to assimilation within the fascist project. There are no limits to the representational logic of fascist discourse.

Schwarz (1986, p.185), however, has criticised this type of approach. He argues that the limits of ideological discourse lie not only in the imaginative inventiveness of ideologues but also in the historical specificity of their cultural resources, 'the weight of tradition' and its language. That is, a connotative resonance between say, a political discourse and its cultural environment, will depend on the symbolic resources which that situation has to offer. The implication here is that meaning is sedimented in the cultural resources, rather than autonomously generated by chains of signifiers. It would be of little avail, for example, to propound economic liberalism in a society where ideas on distribution are based on reciprocity rather than market forces.

Callinicos (1982, p.29) remarks that the effect of Saussure's work is to lift language off reality. It has been argued in this chapter (see also Chapter 6) that such a separation need not be entertained precisely because language, as discursive practice, is itself an attribute of the material world. On this view it is not possible to prise apart language and the world.

The signifier-signified split, absolutised by the absence of a context of meaning utterance entails that semiotics, taken on its own, relativises and subjectivises meaning. This view can be contrasted with Frege's (Dummett, *op. cit.*, p.132) assertion that meaning, as the sense of an utterance, is a characteristic of the world rather than being subjective in the way of referring purely to how people interpret or make cognitive associations between things.

The phenomenological significance of connotation resides in its 'background' quality. It is what is communicated without actually being put in the form of definition; its terms are meaningful, and yet they remain undefined (see sections on Ricoeur and Russell). As a taken for granted basis of judgements/actions, connotation operates in the way of a fund of cultural presuppositions which over-determine or articulate the symbols and signs in communication processes. This can be illustrated by showing how forms of signification, such as those in advertising, which claim to stand in their own right, are in fact dependent for their meanings on a cultural 'undertow'.

The use of irony in contemporary advertising evokes a sense or posture of detachment, a kind of knowingness. Postmodern irony is a kind of 'blank' irony, which is to irony what *pastiche* is to parody - it substitutes nostalgia for critical reflexivity (Jameson, 1991, p.17). This postmodern form of sensibility relies on what Jameson (*op. cit.*, p.20), following Barthes (1975), has referred to as intertextuality. The advert does not refer in the first place to an order of reality but to another text. The contemporaneous use of images of women to sell cars refers to the text of women-as-car-sales-prop in the fifties and sixties. However, what makes the ironic point here is not the suggested *difference* between the two texts, although there is a difference, but rather the covert appeal to the 'what we all know' of the cultural background. In other words, without the sexist connotations embedded in the advert's contextualisation, it would have no point. The base line of the connotative context here is that it is o.k. to use women to sell cars, and this is accomplished by mobilising a whole chain of connotations from the cultural background about female representation and role which reinforce and complexify this point.

An image that appears to hinge on difference and ironic detachment in fact relies on resemblance with the taken for granted to get the contrast in its images going. This suggests that the meaning of signs goes beyond those differentially related signifying structures themselves.

The implication here for cultural background, the intersubjective dimension of social life, is that it is anything but 'background'. The fact that the intertextual comment is structured by this taken for granted suggests it has a far more active and 'extratextual' symbolic character (indicating the way the text is 'done', received) than is traditionally allowed by, for example, the Schutzian model of the taken for granted as 'we-ness'. This indicates a fund of ideas - typical constructs - that can be drawn upon in guiding the construction of social order (Schutz, *op. cit.*, p.7ff). In this discussion, the taken for granted is seen not so much as a bank of disembodied cultural constructs, but rather as embodied in social relations, structures or systems through which individuals act and are constituted. That is, intersubjectivity is embodied because the culture is always *practised*. The connotative, symbolic character of the taken for granted is extratextual in this sense of *active embodiment*.

Ricoeur and Semiotics: From Metaphor to Metaphysics

So far, connotation has been discussed in relation to its systematising function and, via metaphor, as a means of characterising the production of meaning coherence in the social world. The discussion now turns to examine the linguistic processes through which connotation functions within the metaphorical image. Needless to say, it will be argued that the mechanisms of language involved here are not purely linguistic in some abstract sense but have a materialist side too. Hence, understanding the working of metaphor will also serve to illuminate the brief account of Laclau's views on the symbolic constitution of social formations via connotation.

However, Laclau's typification of discourse in terms of a syntagmatic combination and paradigmatic displacement is challenged by Ricoeur's suggestion (see below) that these are not the separate processes indicated in Saussure and Jakobson. Rather, Ricoeur suggests, displacement involves combination; when one terms stands for another, it does so only by taking on the meaning given to the first term by its language context, not the meaning due to one free-standing sign/signification replacing another. On this view, the resultant is a displacement made possible through the acknowledgement that the limits of its role are determined by the meaning context, the context of utterance.

In his analysis of language, Riceour (1986, p.4) crucially distinguishes between (a) a semiotics, where the word as it stands in isolation is treated as being governed by lexical codes for its connotative value, for example, the connotative codes given in 'ordinary usage'; (b) a semantics, where the sentence is taken to be the bearer of the minimum unit of complete meaning. Ricoeur argues that a problem with structural and poststructural linguistics is that it does not distinguish between semiotics and semantics, or more precisely, it considers such a distinction to be improper and reductively pursues a 'monism of the sign' (*ibid.*, pp.101-2, 124).

Ricoeur (*op. cit.*, p.66) further suggests that different theories of metaphor parallel the semiotic and semantic approaches to meaning referred to above. These are respectively the substitution and interaction theories. In an interactive view of metaphor, meaning depends on an interaction between proper and figurative meaning. Ricoeur argues that this is relevant at the level of discourse because at this level of language denotation or reference to objects takes place. The substitution approach, on the other hand, operates at the level of the movement or displacement of meaning within words. The substitution theory is valid, it is argued, because isolated words *do* remain effective carriers of meaning, that is, they have a *rhetorical* effect [power of sedimented meanings]. However, the significance of semiotic theories of meaning is limited to this. Semiotic meaning proves to be a kind of shorthand for other meaning-generating processes. Ricoeur (*op. cit.*, p.217) argues that a more productive approach is to look at the function which a statement as a whole carries in relation to producing meaning in the individual word.

A further move in this argument is to oppose the suggestion found in Derridean linguistics that all language is figurative; that the distinction between figurative and proper meaning in language use is illegitimate and therefore that reference has no stability. The criticism here is that Derrida's

(1974, p.31) argument that proper or literal meaning is really 'dead metaphor' and hence smuggles in something unsaid, invisible, mistakes the role of the proper.[2]

In denotation, following the Frege-Dummett perspective, for a moment, the literal or proper does not itself denote, but rather provides a linguistic formulation, a convention through which meaning can be framed within the context in which a conversation occurs. Hence, what is denoted depends on the context of utterance, rather than literal description. The literal, descriptive phrase as convention, sedimented meaning is already articulated in the context of utterance, and hence predicated.

The crucial break with tradition here is that the subject and its predicate do not exist in linguistic practice as separate entities - there is no proper *per se*. Their separation is a consequence of our abstractional abilities. Consequently, there is nothing invisible about the dead metaphor, it takes its meaning from the context of utterance, not in platonic isolation. Why the literal as convention is seen as separate is a question of reification and as such falls amongst many others. In sum, semiotics, as the treatment of terms in isolation from context of use, ignores the interdependence of conventional and metaphorical meaning.

As against the reductiveness of the semiotic account of meaning, Ricoeur (*op. cit.*, p.34) cites Aristotle's view that metaphor represents a process of actualisation, the coming to be of a genus, not a transcendental reality. The contrast here is between language as an autonomous sign system - which must itself raise questions about invisible moving forces - and language as discursive practice, language as activity which goes beyond language itself to express a coming-into-being; here metaphor is both mimesis and (poetic-creative) *phusis* (*ibid.*, pp.42-3).

Following this brief summary of Ricoeur's views on metaphor, it will pay to examine some of his arguments around connotation more closely.

Ricoeur and Substitution: Jakobson, Laclau, Mouffe

Ricoeur (*op. cit.*, p.177) notes that the post-Saussurian Jakobson's (1971) work splits types of linguistic process into an opposition between metonymy and metaphor. His work on the language disorder area of aphasia showed that these processes could function independently. In one aphasic disorder, people found difficulty in showing that one kind of thing was like another. In another sort of aphasia, substituting terms for each other could be achieved but the trope of continuity in speech, the successful linking of thoughts, disappeared. Jakobson (*op. cit.*, p.243) concluded that the metonymic processes of association in the unfolding of a speech act were independent of those processes related to use of simile. Ricoeur argues that although it may be true that these tropes of language operate independently, it does not follow that the *logical* structure of the two processes is completely different.

Ricoeur notes that whilst Jakobson uses a traditional definition of metaphor as substitution of one term by another with which it is connected by similarity, a parallel structure could be discerned in metonymic processes such as the association of words, sentences or parts of a sentence. This could be described as 'a substitution of names' (*ibid.*, p.179). An example of this would be Jakobson's own illustration of metonymy taken from Tolstoy's *War and Peace*, where the term 'bare shoulders' comes to stand for 'women at a ball'.

On the other hand, quoting Jakobson on the essence of metaphor as presenting 'an idea under the sign of another idea that is more striking or better known', Ricoeur argues that this 'procedure consist[s] as much in combining as in substituting' (*ibid.*, p.180). Hence, it is not clear that the substituting function of language can be isolated from the combinative (metonymic) function. It is unsatisfactory to accept Jacobson's view that 'the meaning of a sign is the sign it can be translated into'; that, in sum, meaning is obtained when 'we substitute signs'.

Ricoeur (*op. cit.*, pp.129-31) goes on to argue, following Benveniste (1971), that meaning occurs in a context, that words acquire meaning via discourse, work, institutionalisation. This reduces the polysemy or play of meaning and enables speakers to have semantic compatibility, to share a common meaning and hence pick out, identify, refer to, things.

The idea of a discursive context suggests that meaning occurs where something is said about something else and that meaning cannot be reduced beyond this to the level of signs standing on their own. In other words, meaning always requires a subject and a predicate, as follows: 'The sky [subject] is blue' [predicate]. This is not simply a combination of names because there is a connotative force between 'sky' and 'blue'. Whilst the connotation is clear in this sentence, in others it may not be. For example, there is no such meaning overlap in 'The key was left at the house on the corner,' taken as such. Now, if the structuralist, semiotic approach were taken in this instance, the sentence or its elements would be seen in isolation and the connections would appear to be purely metonymic/contingent. However, a way round this would be to view the sentence as part of a text or discourse where its elements can take on resonant meanings. If the house on the corner is occupied by a friend of the person who has left the key and picking up the key is an accepted practice as a means of access to another house for people who have been informed of the statement, then 'key' and 'house on the corner' have some meaning overlap. Hence, within the context of a bundle of other statements, there is a connotative overdetermination of the first statement which consequently functions metaphorically.

From this contextualisation of a statement it would seem that *language in general functions metaphorically*. That is, apart from its conventional sense, any statement must also be seen as semantically overdetermined by a field of connotations. Hence, according to the Frege-Dummett view (Dummett, *op. cit.*, p.177), the sentential context constitutes a field of reference and by over-determining the conventional meaning of its subject (name) the sentence picks out a state of affairs, a reality. The tendency to identify literal or proper meaning with the denotative reference, is, notes Frege, a mistake (*ibid.*, p.57). This goes some way towards the semiotic rejection of reference. However, Frege's point is not that reference cannot reach beyond language but that to describe or pick out a state of affairs requires the overdetermination of conventional meaning of the subject/name by sentential sense, the plurality of nuances present in the context of utterance.

Hence, the work of Benveniste and Frege might amplify the point made by Ricoeur that the determination of meaning works ultimately at the level of text or discourse.

To summarise: whatever the interaction between different processes in language, it can be said for the sentence, as for the semiotic juxtaposition of terms, that a metaphorical relation exists between the elements. In other words, one element stands for, displaces, the other, but does not exhaust its meaning. In both cases the metaphorical force owes something to a wider context of signs and statements, that is, they comprise a field of connotation vis-à-vis the metaphor.

If we move on to the question of reference raised by Frege we find that whilst the account of discursivity in Laclau (1987) and Laclau and Mouffe (1989) at the beginning seems to be an advance on previous accounts of the coherence of ideologies or discourses, it also suffers the weaknesses of Foucauldian, and post-Saussurian structuralism in that it cannot move beyond names and meaning conventions. The consequence of this semiotic perspective is that any denotative function of language is collapsed into the metaphorical-connoting function; there is no discursive context of metaphor within which the latter can refer, no distinction à la Frege (1952, pp.57-8), between sense and reference. It is therefore now appropriate to examine how these two functions may be distinguished in language. That is, Ricoeur's argument that the metaphoricity of language does not preclude a denoting, identifying function will be pursued through a classic statement of the compatibility of non-literal and denotative functions.

The Theory of Descriptions

Russell's (1973) Theory of Descriptions indicates two types of non-contradictory function in a sentence, the metaphorical functioning of language and the denotative or identifying function. This contrasts with Laclau's semiotic approach where metaphorical evocation of meaning is the key element and the possibility of reference or aboutness of discourse is undermined by the lack of a meaning context showing how language is used. By contrast, in following Russell, it is possible to delineate a classifying, denoting function within the sentential structure without loss of metaphoricity in the context of utterance.

Russell looks at the way descriptive phrases (names) work within a statement to refer or denote. He argues that if we accept the traditional idea of denotation, that first there is a conceptual object which we then subject to classification, then the result is a kind of Platonism or nominalism, where we subordinate reality to our concepts. As we have suggested, semiotic meanings, fixed within binary oppositions come to exemplify this both in their structuralist and poststructuralist variants (see Chapter 6). To support his criticism of nominalism, Russell looks at the paradoxes which arise if we assume the traditional position that referring is the straightforward business described above, that is, subject and predicate are firstly separate and then brought together in an act of predication. The paradoxes can be illustrated as follows. Suppose we are set the task of deriving as many words as possible from the formulation 'Chinese New Year', then someone might suggest adding 'Chinese New Year' to the list. If Chinese New Year is taken as one of the permutations in the class of words derivable then it contains all the other permutations, so it cannot be one of the permutations. On the other hand, if Chinese New Year is not a permutation of itself then it contains all the permutations, which includes itself. Therefore it is a member of itself.[3]

For Russell, the solution to such paradoxes lies in the nature of descriptive (denoting) phrases. Descriptions like 'Chinese New Year' or 'the author of *Waverley*', Russell (1973, pp.105, 108 f.2) argues, 'never have any meaning in themselves'. They do not designate an individual (entity) directly. They carry a meaning only by virtue of the symbolic (propositional) context. Hence, the descriptive phrases like 'the round square' or 'the golden mountain', although metaphorical, do not involve a contradiction between, for example, 'mountain' (separate subject) and 'golden' (separate predicate) because the subject-predicate relationship does not comprise two separate entities. Frege (Carl, 1994, pp.63-6), on whom Russell is relying here for the denotation-meaning distinction, remarked that we mistake the *syntax* of subject-predicate for the more liberal way subjects are actually formed. Concepts are not separate objects. Rather there is one entity, that which is identified, denoted by the sentential context of the statement. Hence concepts used in utterances are situated by the context and in referring via the sentence do not have a conventional or abstract meaning.

Russell (*op. cit.*, p.105) argues that ultimately statements depend for their ability to denote something on definite descriptions, e.g. 'the author of *Waverley*' which in conjunction with a proper name, e.g. 'Scott', identify an individual. Here, the meaning of the proper name 'Scott' is not determined by the words of the statement 'Scott is the author of Waverley' itself, but by knowing to whom the name is applied. The meaning of the utterance depends on our being acquainted directly with its basic, implicit claims, for example, who Scott is. Therefore in the Theory of Descriptions, Russell had come to acknowledge that descriptions on their own were not logical entities which denoted, but only became meaningful in terms of the sentential context of their use (Monk, 1996, p.182).[4] This included forms of taken for granted knowledge, 'knowledge by acquaintance', or what phenomenologists might refer to as background assumptions.[5]

Denotation, Connotation and the Place of Contradiction

Now as we have seen, the Theory of Descriptions suggests that it is possible to have both denotative and connotative functions in discourse without engendering some kind of contradiction and incoherence in reference itself - although we can maintain a place for contradiction, nevertheless. Dummett's (*op. cit.*, p.177) elaboration of this Fregean tradition suggests that there are two forms of reference in the sentential utterance: that the sentence expresses a state of affairs, and hence we might suppose, *with all its contradictions*; it also denotes or picks out a object, event, etc., that is, has referential capacity.

Language is the site of contradiction, in that the sense of an utterance - the state of affairs expressed - can be articulated in different ways (Russell, *op. cit.*, p.108), and so come to be embodied in different statements which contest its referential import by picking out different objects. Any one statement has itself, however, a clear (non-contradictory) denotative potential (*loc. cit.*). This obviously has consequences for how we view the rationality of everyday life and its discourses, as these discourses will consequently not just include myth, stereotypes, ossified practice but will contain denotative potential. Hence, our sense of the epistemological status of everyday language will have to be revised.

The valorisation of overtly metaphorical language as a site of contestation over reference enables us to see metaphor as the condensation of different fields of reference, and hence connotation, and therefore to incorporate the semiotic concerns around contradiction (condensation/ displacement). However, the state of affairs expressed in metaphorical language is expressed via the situated *use* of language, and this takes us further than semiotics can travel on its own. This is because the meaningfulness (coherence) of language rests on a capacity to pick out states of affairs rather than on a sign user's substitution of signs according to predetermined meaning conventions; the meaning of 'Scott' in 'Scott is the author of Waverley' rested not on the words of the statement itself, but on the sense given by context, which tells us to whom the name is applied. It is this anchoring of reference in the meaning context of signification which can, in Frege's (Carl, *op. cit.*, p.53) terms, *break the power of words*.

Notes

1   In this, the notion of realism here differs from *transcendental* accounts of realism.
2   Derrida, following Heidegger, holds that metaphor, and hence all language, is metaphysical being motivated by an invisible transcendental signified (Ricoeur, *op. cit.*, p.34).
3   This illustration is inspired by Monk's account of the 'class of all classes' paradox which taxed Russell over a period of years and to which the Theory of Descriptions offered a solution (Monk, 1996, pp.182-3).
4   Russell is thought to owe this insight to the U.S. mathematician Maxime Bôcher, who wrote to him 'I cannot admit that a class is in itself an entity...the "class as one [class itself]" is merely a symbol, a *name* which we may choose at pleasure' (Monk, *op. cit.*, p.183).

5   As he took Frege's 'sense' to be a kind of object, Russell rejected that aspect (sense determines reference) of Frege's argument about denotation, believing it would lead to a form of idealism. He substituted knowledge by acquaintance, direct, uncogitated knowing, as a way of grounding abstract knowledge in direct apprehension of things (Dummett, *op. cit.*, pp.130-132). It is possible to interpret this as a kind of phenomenological position where what is 'bracketed' or taken for granted knowledge provides a context for denotation.

5 Sense and Reference: The Everyday as Basis and Critique of Classification Systems

The aim of this chapter is to examine a variety of notions of sense and reference, ranging from Husserl's phenomenology through to recent views on representation in cultural studies. The implications of these positions for establishing an account of intersubjectivity are investigated.

Husserl and the Life-World

For Husserl, the activities of everyday life are characterised as the domain of the life-world (*Lebenswelt*). This is seen as a realm of pre-theoretical life out of which science is constructed by abstraction from everyday beliefs. The life-world is revealed to us by a process of bracketing (epoche) of our taken for granted beliefs about the world ('natural attitude') (Husserl, 1970, p.135). As with Frege (see below), an attempt is made to isolate *noema* or pure meanings, however, Frege locates the objectivity of meaning in actual language structures (Dummett, *op. cit.*, p.54) whilst Husserl lapses into transcendentalising the real and hence making it accessible only via psychologistic means (*ibid.*, p.59).

Hence for Husserl (*op. cit.*, p.50), the life-world is the original ground of all theoretical and practical life - the immediately intuited world; it is the world actually given through perception. Hence it is a pre-cognitive domain ('of things unknown'), it is open-ended unlike the self-referencing, 'closed' abstractions and idealities of theory (*loc. cit.*, f. 9d). In the world of theory, on the other hand, Husserl follows Galileo's mathematical methodology, which produces idealisations from empirical knowledge, implies the perfection of knowledge, and so departs from empirical reality (*ibid.*, p.121).

The Cartesian pre-given ego is the starting point for Husserl's theory of intersubjectivity. The world is given in experience to the individual subject who then transforms it via the categories of logic and language into an intersubjective form. The problem this raises for Husserl is how consciousness can recognise the reality conveyed by pure experience. The implication here is that language structures are already given for the *individual* subject and therefore that experience itself already takes the form of a categorial intuition (*ibid.*, No. vi, Chapter 8). Now the present argument is that whilst Husserl is right to suggest that experience, and hence the *Lebenswelt*, is a categorialised, discursive entity, he fails to see this as a feature of an intersubjective - not individual - subject. Husserl also seems correct in characterising experience as bivalent: on the one hand it is private and unique in the sense that it is given to individuals, but at the same time it embodies social categories such as language and logic. Hence, a dual moment of connection or intersubjectivity and individualisation of social beings would seem to be required. The sticking point for Husserl here would be the requirement for non-individual intersubjective location of ideas. This goes against his insistence on the primacy of individual consciousness. The necessity of the latter claim for Husserl resides in his establishment of consciousness itself as the ground of intersubjectivity. It follows that intersubjectivity must be located within individual consciousness (Husserl, 1960, p.104). Thus the individual appears to be both the substance/content and ground of knowledge - a move which guarantees the unity of the individual subject, but at the expense of ignoring the fragmentary, decentered character of experience.

Hence Husserl faces the same problems that bedevilled Descartes, that is, the pitfalls of mind-body dualism. Husserl's reply to the question 'How can one know the other?' is that this can only occur by analogy. One can only know the other by drawing parallels with one's own bodily states. The fact that the subject itself requires an already categorialised experience which forms the basis of linguistic practices and hence knowledge/individual consciousness, is passed over in the attempt to preserve the integrity of the subject.

The unity of the subject is effected transcendentally, that is, in the realm of pure experience (and transcendental phenomenology). Consequently, Husserl sacrifices the whole of material nature; he refuses to accept the structure of reality as it is given in experience prior to epoche as intersubjectively valid and thereby loses a point of reference in the real world. However, as Habermas (1970, p.40) notes, the importance of

Husserl for the development of a theory of intersubjectivity lies in his identification of the life-world as the basis of theoretical knowledge:

> the possible objects of scientific knowledge have already constituted themselves beforehand in the phenomena which our common-sense world [*Lebenswelt*] takes for granted...Thus Husserl wishes to show that this active subjectivity is lost sight of under the cover of an objectivist taking-things-for granted...

albeit that Husserl wishes to reinstate this contemplative posture at the level of pure experience! The important point then is that Husserl has broken with reflection or correspondence theories of knowledge (and reference) at the empirical level. That is to say, if his position here is followed through, it entails giving up the traditional or classical view of knowledge and reference wherein ideas are a copy of an external reality. The theme of reference will be expanded later in the section on language and classification.

The work of Alfred Schutz (cf. *The Phenomenology of the Social World*, and Chapter 2 of this work, for instance) takes up Husserl's view that in the empirical world theoretical knowledge is intersubjectively founded. Schutz's writing develops the application of Husserl's ideas to the social world, but whereas Husserl was concerned with theorising the possibility of pure experience and the bracketing (epoche) of the taken-for-granted everyday world, Schutz (1970a) brackets the concern with pure experience and concentrates on the characteristics of the everyday world.

Unfortunately, Schutz reproduces Husserl's Cartesian view of the empirical world, where he divides the Other into knowable object (for me) and unknowable subject.

> My unknown neighbour in the subway is defined by my knowing him as being in New York, travelling in such and such a direction, reading his newspaper...the objectified Other is...determined by the total organisation of *my* world, of which he is an autonomous but intra-mundane center. This distinguishes the Other as an object from the Other as a subject. Only the former can be known to me as a co-extensive totality within the world. The latter can never be an object of any kind of knowledge, and the objects of the world do not refer to him; he transcends the world...' (Schutz, 1967, p.190).

The major difficulty with this perspective is that it assumes a pre-given 'me', a centre in terms of which 'the world' is then organised but for whose pre-existing unity there is no explanation.

Habermas

Another application of the Husserlian life-world perspective is found in the work of Jurgen Habermas. However, whilst Husserl links objectivity with transcendental consciousness, Habermas sees intersubjectivity as operating through the structures of language and communication after the manner of Husserl's categorial intuition of pure experience. In Habermas the categories of communication provide the deep (ideal) structures of objective knowledge, whilst for Husserl such categorial intuitions are non-objective because they belong to the experiential life-world (out of which ideal structures of knowledge must somehow be created).

Habermas (1970, p.48) rejects the ontology implicit in the Husserlian project and argues that objectivity can be situated in an elucidation of the conditions under which communication can be effective, that is, the 'free dialogue of all with all' is the condition of 'a mutually formed self-identity'. However, all knowledge claims are interest-based, and intersubjectivity replaces subjectivity in a dualism of objective world v. knowledge as Komesaroff (1986, p.363) argues. Habermas's emphasis on the ability of individuals to apply intersubjective 'depth grammar' in their interactions illustrates the extent to which the life-world in Habermas is accessible to individual consciousness, and therefore, as with Husserl, appears as an extension of the latter rather than something qualitatively different. In a similar vein (and category mistake), the validity claims made in communication belong at the same time to the worlds of individual consciousness and intersubjectivity as they are geared to *intersubjective recognition* (my emphasis - H.F.) if their rationality is to be upheld (Habermas, 1991, p.314).

Furthermore, speakers' utterances relate to 'something in the objective world, something in a common social world and something in his [*sic*] own subjective world' (*ibid.*, pp.313-4). Hence, intersubjectivity is still counterposed to an ideal or objective domain beyond it. These illustrations bear out the suggestion above, that for Habermas intersubjectivity and subjectivity seem to be functionally interchangeable, whilst it has been the case of the present author that the intersubjective world *is* the social world.

As with Husserl, Habermas's argument assumes that the subject predates or anticipates the world of which it must be an interactive and therefore mutually constitutive element. The conditions of its possibility can only be given in interaction and yet it somehow *already* knows the interactive process.

Everyday Objects: The Irredeemably Contextual Nature of Reference

Now Frege's approach to meaning is implicitly a theory of intersubjectivity, that is, its 'context principle' illuminates the issue of shared meaning as a basis for the communicability of statements.[1] In contrast to the earlier Husserl who located meaning ultimately in the transcendental consciousness of individual minds by a process of bracketing out the background cultural aspects, Frege locates meaning via the context principle in his discussion of fixing the references of numerical terms in the *Grundlagen* (Dummett, *op. cit.*, pp.424-5). He rejects the idea that sense of utterances about numerical terms must reflect fixed references for numbers, in favour of only arriving at a reference for numbers as an outcome of sentential context. Hence sentential utterances only work via an understanding of their constituent meanings/senses, how they are articulated within the utterance and how the whole of that relates to the present context, that within which the utterance takes place (*ibid.*, p.444). Hence meaning is something irredeemably shared. He reinforces this point by stressing that the senses of utterances are not events in individual consciousnesses, that is not mental contents. Rather they are objective entities, which in Dummett's reading arise in the process of picking out objects in our utterances, that is, the sense of an utterance is given by the manner in which or, the *practice* of, identifying its object (*ibid.*, pp.444-5). The idea that reference can be fixed *a priori*, that is, that a name stands for an object without reference to context of shared meanings is to invoke a vicious circularity where the question of what an utterance picks out becomes undecidable.

The emphasis in Dummett's interpretation of Frege is on linguistic practice, rather than the (rhetorical) effects of names or language *per se*.

> [Frege's] context principle expressly denies that there can be any grasp of the reference of a name antecedently to an ability to understand or use sentences containing it: it is only in the context of a sentence that a name even has a reference (*ibid.*, p.347).

Dummett (*op. cit.*, p.461) points out that even in cases of what appear to be a straightforward referral to objects, the empirical 'this is one of those' type of statement, reference is still a hermeneutic event. Such a reference

> involves a description of the most basic layer of language, that in which demonstratives play an essential role, which...is a complex matter; we

cannot explain what it is to treat a name as standing for an object of a certain kind without explaining what it is to identify an object of that kind.

This grasping the sense of an utterance is accomplished in the manner described above and involves, in Dummett's view, the distribution of a mental act beyond the individual mind to encompass the context, thus demonstrating its objectivity (*loc. cit.*).

Dummett's notion of objectivity here is tied into the way context informs 'the most basic layer of language' and this returns us to Husserl's theme that knowledge is founded in the everyday. The indexical nature of the basic layer of language contains all those routinised events and processes, the everyday dimension of communication which can operate more or less independently of explicit knowledge claims. Dummett (*op. cit.*, pp.445-6) shows via Wittgenstein's examples that people can function communicatively by grasping the sense of affairs under discussion - language use itself is a prime case of this. They may or may not be able to make explicit reference to the processes in hand. Denotative reference therefore follows from grasping the sense of events, but not vice versa. The explicit identification of objects - empirical or otherwise - depends in the first place on the most basic level of language, the sphere where routinisation renders reference opaque. The point here is that the denotative, propositional expression of reference remains tied to the sentential context where it arises as it shares the same sense.[2] The descriptive phrases or names of the utterance are articulated within this context and their *explicit* or conventionalised content is therefore determined by the shared contextual knowledge *implicit* within the sentence.

The conception of knowledge development entailed here differs sharply from Hegel's *aufhebung* or positive negation in that for Hegel, a new more developed expression of consciousness encompasses previous stages and they cease to exist independently, there is no remainder in this process. The pivotal role played by senses between context and denotative reference ensures that past references are not subsumed or reinscribed in this way but become sedimented within present utterances as articulations within their overall structure.

Attempts to 'free' non-empirical references from their 'everyday' senses because they do not refer in any obvious way to an object, but rather something less tangible or coherent (Ricoeur, *op. cit.*, p.221ff) are doomed to fail, as Dummett argues even for the case of arithmetical numbers. Ricoeur's (*op. cit.*, p.230) suggestion that in such cases reference is incoherent confuses the aspects of how reference is achieved (giving sense) with the incoherence of the object referred to (reference). Literary or other manifestly metaphorical topics would constitute abstract objects (and none the less real for that, if they 'made sense') whose nature could be described via a hermenutics of the context, which would elucidate their everyday articulations with explicit content. Giving abstract objects a separate sense from that of context would merely serve to perpetuate a circular process where conversants could not appeal to a *common* context.

The question of everyday as critique is a culmination of the foregoing considerations in that everyday functioning involves grasping senses of topics if not their objectified forms. It involves (actively) making sense. We turn now to examine this trope of communication.

A Critique of Discursive Classification in Laclau and Mouffe

The stress of discourse-orientated approaches, such as that of Foucault, is on the employment of language as a tool of subjection, and both its theoretical and reflexive characteristics are ignored. Cultural commentators including Foucault, Laclau and Mouffe emphasise only the instrumental capacity of language as a form of power. The possibility of subjects acting as conscious rational agents is neglected. However, this latter point is also levelled against earlier phenomenological commentators such as Schutz, in their use of the concept 'everyday life' (cf. Heller, 1984, xi-xii).

Whilst the rationality of individuals goes unrecognised, discourse theorists nevertheless examine the patterned features of discourses and their articulation. Laclau (1989, p.105ff), for example, sees discourses as constituted out of an articulation of elements, the different spheres of social practice - familial, educational, economic, etc. The articulation represents a 'moment', a degree of fixity, in which the elements are configured or patterned such that the configuration has an overall logic of its own in which the elements connote each other to the exclusion of other symbolic entities, those not configured within the symbolic formation of, for example, a particular ideology. Now, arguably, such discursive formations constitute particulars in the classical Leibnizian sense of 'active principles of unity' (Hacking, 1970, p.146ff). They represent a bundle of predicates unified by a common logic, and as such constitute a material form of force.

However, whilst such discursive-material entities populate the social world, they themselves contain other material entities, Laclau argues. He gives the example of the process of building. The linguistic practices involved are as material as are the bricks themselves: discourse consists of 'diverse material elements' (Laclau & Mouffe, 1989, p.108). He notes that there is a 'prejudice' about the 'mental character of discourse' and wishes to 'affirm the material character of every discursive structure'. Further, 'What constitutes a differential position [within a discourse] and therefore a relational identity, is not the idea of building stone or slab, but the building stone or slab as such' (*loc. cit.*). Hence Laclau's use of 'ideas' does not carry the weight of being materially discursive which is suggested by his comments on the materiality of articulations of discursive practices, and in fact it reproduces the mind-body problem within discourse. The difficulty lies in the assimilating of physically extended things such as slabs, to a world of discursive or ideational features, because in doing so the writers make an elision between physically extended things and 'the material'. Now Collier (1991, pp.89-90) has argued that ideas and physically extended attributes of things are not to be treated as separate entities, but as attributes of the same thing. The brick, for example, already has a sedimented meaning as, for example, building block/unit, prior to articulation within a specific discourse. Further, the physically extended attribute and the idea, of the brick, for example, are not assimilated to the same causal situations because they represent different attributes of matter and such an assimilation would involve a category mistake. For example, we cannot drop an idea on our toes, although we can appreciate or wrestle with it.

With this in mind let us return to Laclau and Mouffe's theory of discourse. The function of 'idea' in the building process example is as a reflection of the real thing, the slab, which is seen as a *non-discursive* content of discourse! Hence ideas revert to their traditional function as separate from and, as in correspondence theories, constituting mental reflections of matter. The re-emergence of dualism in Laclau and Mouffe's discourse theory is not accidental to their project, because they fail to accept that materiality of ideas gives them an 'independent', that is, non-subjectivised existence and this leads them to treat physical entities as non-discursive because a discursive existence would subjectivise them!

In sum, the theory is too parsimonious and fails to account for the reality of sedimented meanings. In terms of Dummett's context principle, the theory attributes names directly to objects without consideration of the mediating sense in the meaning context, which, in the Frege-Dummett approach, has its own material efficacy.

Language or Communicative Practice?: A Constitutive Ambiguity in Cultural Commentary

The role of meaning in contemporary cultural analysis tends to oscillate between a semiotic, pre-given structure of signification and a more phenomenological, negotiated, contextual, layered conception. The influence of Laclau and Mouffe is substantial in Hall (ed.) (1997) and du Gay (ed.) (1997), but the counterpoint to this is some context - technological tradition, diasporic sedimentation, etc. Du Gay's (1997) study of the origins and uses of the Walkman is a classic illustration of the importance of a particular tradition to the process of 'making sense'. Hall's (Rutherford ed., 1990; Woodward ed., 1997)) account of language transmission through diaspora is likewise seminal.

On the other hand, the semiotics of language tend, themselves, to get *decontextualised*. In this mode, language inclines to take off on its own. For example, in arguing for a Foucauldian perspective, Hall (1997, p.44) notes:

> By discourse Foucault meant a group of statements which provide a language for talking about - a way of representing the knowledge about - a particular topic at a particular historical moment...Discourse is about the production of knowledge through language...

Discourse tends to be about 'language', 'classification', construction of objects, writing - or the inscription of discourse on bodies. In Foucault, for example, 'the body' is 'radically historicized',

> a sort of surface on which different regimes of power/knowledge write their meanings and effects. It thinks of the body as totally imprinted by history (Hall, in Hall ed., 1997, p.51).

Here language is already sedimented meaning, never the moment at which meaning *comes to be* via language *use*. As Hall further notes, for Derrida 'writing always leads to more writing' (*ibid.*, p.42), that is an on-going process of the dissemination of meaning. In Derrida's terms, meaning is always retreating from us, always already sedimented, a transcendental signified, rather than seen as incarnated in the moment of its actualisation.

Again, Hall presenting Foucault's account of madness:

> [it was] constituted by all that was said, in all the statements that named it, divided it up, described it, explained it, traced its development, indicated its various correlations, judged it, and possibly gave it speech by articulating, in its name, discourses that were to be taken as its own (Foucault, 1972, in Hall, *op. cit.*, p.46).

Finally, following Lacau and Mouffe (1990. pp.102-3), Hall (*op. cit.*, p.47) argues that a stone may be a projectile or a piece of sculpture, depending on the type of discourse it enters, and that it has no meaning beyond its positioning within discourse. Now Dummett has argued that the constituents of utterances carry their own senses given by previous context of utterance, sedimented within the present utterance. Hence the objects or topics referred to in previous enunciation are incorporated in current communication. In this crucial respect, although the parsimony of representation theory disallows it, meaning certainly exists outside discourse. That is, the names given to objects in discourse theories supposedly refer directly and not via the context, as there is no term to represent contextual meaning over and against conventional meaning.

Now, as argued above and in Chapter 4, theories of direct referencing (via conventional meanings) produce insuperable difficulties for establishing the meaning of objects. As above, establishing the name of the object involves an infinite regress of appeal via reference to other objects in a chain of definition or substitution of terms as there is no shared meaning context to arbitrate what the object is, referentially.

Further, Russell's (1973, p.109) Paradox establishes that to consider names and objects, as per subject and predicate, to be separate entities results in a contradiction. That is, in order to be named, an object must already be recognised as coming under the name and conversely, if the object already has the name then it cannot come under the name. This demonstrated to Russell and others (cf. Monk, 1996) that the traditional view of naming was seriously flawed, or in our view, too parsimonious.

The Everyday as Interruption and Transfiguration

Whilst the consideration of meaning as conventional meaning in Foucault and Derrida (see above), that is, as something sutured from the act of utterance conveys a particular impression of sedimentation, that is, as routine and repetition, it is important to see how such 'dead' meaning is reconfigured. That is, the invisible context can be brought to illuminate and revivify 'dead' names, etc. Merleau-Ponty (1992, p.61ff), from the point of view of a theory of perception, describes a kind of *Gestalt* process through which mundane objects take on new meanings. This is the moment of object-in-context, the moment in which we see how everything comes together.

Hence, although names and phrases can be routinely articulated in a kind of repetitive praxis (Heller, 1984), sometimes such conventional meanings can be dramatically transfigured by articulation with another context and sense. This represents a conjunction of different routines. A useful example in 'everyday' culture is the graffiti commentator who modifies adverts. In one such case on the London Underground, a poster advertising the performance-boosting properties of a vitamin potion had the addendum 'It gets you working' which transforms the connotative field from that of individual unlimited performance, with its associations of health and fitness, to that of an employee producing more work output for an organisational superior. All this is achieved by rearticulating the name 'performance' to a different meaning context.

Hence the peculiar nature of the everyday is that one routine series of events can convey a new understanding by its insertion into a different context of routines.[3] The essential point here is that the articulation constitutes an interruption of routine or convention in which we are able to see the routine event in context, i.e. to grasp the sense of a new context of utterance which connects and makes visible the context of the conventionalised advertising phrase via its rearticulation. This moment of the mediation of reference via sense rather than other atomistic terms alone is missing from the semiotic and subsequent poststructuralist account of meaning and representation.

Representation and the Emergence of Reference

As argued above, the traditional reflectionist theories of reference or naming suggested that objects corresponded to, or were constructed by, their names.[4] The alternative picture from within a phenomenological view is that the emergence of entities and names is coincident, that to have a name is also to have an object, real or imaginary, empirical or abstract (Dummett, *op. cit.*, pp.368-9).

The fact that the types of discourse theory examined here relapse into the difficulties around referencing their objects which we have examined above should not, however, detract from the importance of their substantive cultural claims about, for example, the reorganisation of work in recent years. There are clearly institutional discourses bearing on the way subjects act and these are in turn located within wider networks or discursive formations, which have the power to determine the way we think.[5] The problem arises when we ask how this determination operates. The crux is: are names references - whether in the form of semiotic binary terms or otherwise? The difficulty discourse theorists have experienced in formulating a view as to resistance and contestation of meanings is symptomatic of the problem posed above. For reasons investigated here, a basis for resistance could only evolve from some ground which was not itself reducible to a definition of a term and yet the theorists have not identified such a discursive space.

Dummett (*op. cit.*, p.157) poses an answer succinctly when he notes that sense determines reference. The shared contexts of meaning in which we operate with their shared ways of validating discursive claims are always that: they are shared understandings which are not reducible to the way individuals interpret conversational meaning, not coincident with any elaboration, definition, proposition about the conversational content. In his interpretation of social conflict, Merleau-Ponty similarly notes that it is of necessity based upon a communication of meaning; each understands the other - they are bound together intersubjectively in their *encounter*.[6]

The openness of sense to different, *situated* readings allows a terrain for the emergence of genuinely novel meanings and their objects. These are meanings marked by their conditions of production, the context of senses within which they arise. Thus, as Garfinkel notes, the context of enunciation is incorporated into what is *said*, objectified:

> In short, recognisable sense, or fact or methodic character, or impersonality, or objectivity of accounts are not independent of the socially organised occasion of their use. Their rational features consist of what members do with, what they make of the accounts...(*op. cit.*, pp.3-4).

In other words, knowledge here has an irreducibly *practical* basis. In that case, one is left to account for the fetishistic conception meaning entailed in the idea of naming discussed before and perhaps to situate it in the reformalisation or bureaucratisation of social practices consequent on the defeat of a way of doing things associated with the post-1945 settlement. Here the sheer power of discursively formulated information and its sedimentation leaves us with a wall of invisibility surrounding its articulated meanings.

Nonetheless, we can see new meanings as referenced in communicative practices, that is, as actualised, made visible through these practices. As Dummett (*op. cit.*, p.461) notes, regarding the context principle, objects are picked out by a process in which we see how the senses of the constituent phrases of an utterance, its sedimented meanings, are articulated and interact with its conventionalised meaning which is transformed in this process. This is somewhat reminiscent of Merleau-Ponty's *Gestalt* which reveals the object over and against its *field* or contextual articulations and which is thus transfigured towards a new reference.

Ricoeur (*op. cit.*, p.299), in noting the *self-referentiality* of this process of realisation, has observed that when the customary mode of reference fails,

> ...the semantic aim has recourse to a network of predicates that already function in [the] familiar field of reference. This already constituted meaning is raised from its anchorage in an initial field of reference and cast into a new referential field which it will then work to delineate. But this transfer...presupposes that the latter field is already present in a still unarticulated manner, and that it exerts an attraction on the already constituted sense in order to tear it away from its initial haven...this would not be possible if meaning were a stable form.

Hence the stasis which Hall (Hall (ed.), 1997, p.46) criticises in semiotics, and which we have argued is perpetuated in types of discourse theory, results from seeing the process of referencing (and in that sense, naming) as prior to meaning. We have argued that, on the contrary, reference or 'naming' is not prior to but part of the process of actualisation of objects in which reference is shifted as the sense of a context is rendered visible; that objects emerge from communicative practices rather than signs determining their character beforehand.

Notes

[1]   It is important to note that Dummett's use of the term 'intersubjectivity' is quite different from the present meaning. Rather than a world of (shared) senses, for Dummett it implies a disembodied world of shared meanings or experiences as in Lotze's view (*op. cit.*, pp.393-4).

[2]   The (propositional) definition of an indexical expression contains the sense of the latter. This is, Dummett (*op. cit.*, p.340) argues, because we arrive at its truth in the same way as we do for the expression itself. The <u>overall</u> sense of the propositional

utterance will be different from that of the expression it defines, however, because the latter is only a component of the utterance, which by containing it, employs it in a particular way, situates it in a new context. The key point here though is that the sense of the indexical expression is <u>preserved</u>, not reduced to its reformulation. This guarantees the primacy of meaning context over epistemic assimilation in the Hegelian manner.

[3]   Hence particular names or phrases can switch between background and foreground mode, suggesting novel meanings. Heidegger notes this peculiarity in *Being and Time*, when he describes everyday life both in terms of the routine sameness of events and 'diversification' (cited in Osborne, 1995, p.194). It is this quality of *surprise* implied by the latter that marks the revelatory quality of interruption. The everyday is then seen as the point of break or rupture in the everydayness of routine (Lefebvre, 1971, in Osborne, 1995, *loc. cit.*).

[4]   The view taken here is that objects only have names by means of denotative reference and that this depends on the meaning context of the utterances. Hence, the linguistic conventions/names in a sentence only become meaningful via the hermeneutics of denotative reference.

[5]   Du Gay's (1997) discussion of Foucault's notion of governmentality is useful here, particularly in its references to self-regulation and its contemporary relation to discursive figures of 'the entrepreneur'.

[6]   Merleau-Ponty's (1992, p.361) view is of a common (somewhat Heideggerian) ontological basis of subjects intersubjectively related by some form of contestation. This again, as otherwise in the F-D formulation, suggests an opening out of discursive structures to different interpretations of some common form of 'being' or sense, which prevents a monopolisation of power/knowledge.

6 Discursive Realism: Self-Referentiality and the 'Depth' of Meaning

Whilst realism has come under attack from the social constructionists of both modern and postmodern types, the realist response has been to defend a world 'out there'. It will be argued here that the only credible defence of realism lies in firstly accepting that the 'discursive turn' has undermined the world 'out there' position; that there is nothing to which we refer which is not already apart of a system of referencing; and secondly, that this in itself does not necessarily entail a relativism about 'underlying' structures and processes, closure or a self -confirming quality. It will be suggested that the ironic mirroring of our own thoughts, the creation of a world in our own theoretical image, is not the only way of understanding self-referentiality; that the term can equally support a non-mirroring, non-ironic reading which is based on the non-equivalence of referencing categories embedded in the world with those of our own theoretical ideas. Consequently, it is suggested that to accept self-referentiality does not necessitate the abandonment of complexity and depth in communication.

The first part of this chapter looks at some difficulties faced by social constructionist positions in establishing a coherent account of discursivity. Some suggestions will be made as to how these difficulties might be remedied via recognition of a constitutive ambiguity in the structure of a referring discourse. This decisive point is illustrated by means of Dummett's truth conditional semantics, which, it is argued, can serve as a theoretical expression of the alternative account of discursivity, because it distinguishes and theorises a relationship between formal, propositional aspects of discourse on the one hand, and its situatedness in underlying 'everyday' contextual factors of communication, on the other. It recognises that theoretical knowledge is inflected or situated by the manner in which it is arrived at. It is at once both knowledge and discursive practice.

Part 1: The Problem of Embodiment

Mind-Body Dualism: A Contested Characteristic of Contemporary Thought

The position taken here is that ideas are as much a part of the world as physical-spatial structures. As Pivcevic argues, our observations should not be treated as merely reflections on/of the world but as part of the world itself. That is, it is an error to take 'speaking about' (Pivcevic, 1986, p.275) as something separate from the sphere of things being spoken about. The world speaks about itself. Arguably, categories such as 'biological', 'social', 'natural' are illustrations of such a self-referential world in operation.[1] They appear at one and the same time to be both a description and the thing that is being described.

Amongst other writers holding variants of this view, Farrell (1995, p.21) notes that for Hegel understanding requires that:

> our fundamental concepts must capture the world as it is, and even more, must be an explicit actualising of logical patterns that are in some sense present in things and institutions themselves.

Again, for Hegel, the logical relations abstracted from the world 'are not just features of how we look at the world, but are in some sense present in a more primitive form in the very way in which things articulate and exhibit themselves as having a determinate character' (*ibid.*, p.22). We could say, for example, that the structuredness of things has about it a sense of 'how it all fits together', and as such, things themselves contain a 'logic'.[2]

Farrell (*op. cit.*, pp.79-82) goes on to argue that Davidson's radical critique of Quine's relativism - Quine insists that we can put whatever meaning construction we like on aspects of the world - has here in crucial respects a similar outcome. Davidson (1984, pp.227-41) argues that if reference to a world 'out there' truly cannot succeed in identifying things, as Quine (1969, pp.26-68) claims, then such a notion of reference should be abandoned altogether. However, we cannot give up the idea of reference *per se* because even Quine's account of plural worlds requires some grasp of 'what is being referred to'.

For Davidson (*op. cit.*, xix), the consequence of the collapse of 'out there' referencing is not that we abandon the classificatory ideas which count as references to things, but rather that we see them as part of the world. Hence, as Farrell (*op. cit.*, p.90) claims, this is a radically different kind of world from the one Quine demolishes. It is a world in which referencing entails that what is referenced in some sense already has the logical structure of the referring discourse.

The' world out there' view of reference with its privileging of physicalist notions of structures and processes, or again, a material base reflected in ideational superstructures, nevertheless remains influential. This broadly 'base-superstructure' model covers not only variants of Marxism but is more generally current in social theory and has become paradigmatic of the way 'speaking about' has been split off from the world. Hence we tend to see cultural and theoretical structures as reflections of the world. It will be in order to dwell for a moment on the problems posed by base and superstructure and how theorists have attempted to deal with those difficulties.

In Marxism, a tradition was built up of which a core feature was the idea that social being determines consciousness. Now whilst, as Rose (1995, p.215) notes, although Marx argued for a unity of theory and practice, the net effect was to disregard the practice of theory and thus maintain the 'Kantian or Fichtean opposition between theory and practice'. Social life was thus divided into material and ideational factors along the lines of base and superstructure. This mechanical Marxism was later countered by a cultural materialism - Gramsci (1971) and Althusser (1971) for example, which recognised the efficacy of cultural factors such as ideology. The notion that practices were the site of social determination replaced the view of 2nd International Marxism that forces of production or economic laws (technological and economic determinism) were key explanatory factors.

The problem of how to theorise the relationship between practices and ideas nevertheless remained either 'glossed' or unaddressed. Ideas were said to be embodied in institutional practices, the latter were seen as symbolically overdetermined and human agents were seen as the bearers of ideas. Thus the conception of embodiment remained *ad hoc* and bore some similarity to the way in which a currant bun could be said to be the bearer or embodiment of currants.[3] That is, ideas were still seen as discrete entities somehow stuck onto practices rather than practices having an intrinsically ideational quality.[4] (As the examination of Althusser in Chapter 4 suggests, rejection of the base-superstructure metaphor has no necessary consequences for the relative weight of economic influences.)

This problem is again highlighted in the interactionist tradition, where the labelling metaphor is used to explain the self-fulfilling nature of institutional definitions of individuals. The metaphor reproduces the split between the cognitive (label) and bodily elements of agents. Thus, in both the cultural Marxist and the interactionist case, the practice or interaction or individual is seen as a substructure to the ideational/symbolic properties. In this way the base-superstructure metaphor maintains a grip on the theorisation of agency, structure and practice.

The Constitutive Ambiguity of Embodiment

The formulation of ideational embodiment proposed in this discussion is rather different and depends on the argument that laws, structures, logics, relations, plots, narratives, roles - in a word the basic entities through which the world is made sense of - have a dual aspect nature; they exhibit an irreducible ambiguity between being treated as physical/spatial entities and ideational entities. Now, whilst the currant bun figure suggests heterogeneity between physical/spatial and ideational components, the dual aspect notion suggests a gestalt figure where one aspect melts into the other and the two are never entirely separable. Imagine, for example, a line drawing of a cube which reverses itself or an alternating 'two faces/candlestick' diagram. Here, one cannot contemplate one aspect without the other being drawn in, unlike the currents which can easily be conceived in separation from the bun.

Moving on from the cube metaphor, the point can be illustrated by a number of examples. For instance, in a simple 'real world' example, a ball may be said to make or describe an arc or other trajectory. Here, 'describe' etc. refers both to the physical trajectory and to the definition of the shape so 'described'. The shape of its movement, which is understood definitionally or in terms of an ideal type, means that the ball has, in turn, definite physical consequences for a goalkeeper or netball player. The descriptive statement 'The ball made an arc' offers both a description of an event and an account of how it was brought about. According to Garfinkel (*op. cit.*, pp.7-9), all natural language utterances have this 'reflexive', doing/describing character. The one trope is entailed in the other and yet one refers to the 'subjective'/cognitive describing aspect and the other to the 'real world' action aspect if we follow the mind-body dualist perspective. The fact that a description can serve as a comment on how it was brought about was also noted by Spinoza (1986, p.258), when he claimed that defining descriptions always included some reference to how the states of affairs described were brought about, that is, their immediate cause. 'This is a good way of solving Pythagoras' Theorem' would be another example. These two implications of the trajectory or theorem solving - action and description, world and subjectivity - seem indissolubly but puzzlingly linked together. 'Puzzlingly' because the paradigm from which such phenomena are viewed is generally a dualist one, that is, a view in which ideas and bodies or 'the world' are kept in separate compartments.

Farrell (*op. cit.*, p.289) argues from his Hegel and Davidson cases that it is wrong to see thought or reason as placed on one side of a world-subject duality; rather thought should be seen as distributed in both compartments. The idea that thought is solely a characteristic of subjects is, he argues (*ibid.*, p.15), a feature of the 'divinisation' of subjectivity which occurs with the onset of modernity where the subject interprets the world through thoughts which are its own property. Some further illustrations will help to demonstrate the ambiguous nature of thought with regard to the world-subject duality. The ambiguity can, for example, be seen at work in the comment on a building as being 'in the Art Deco style'. Now the building has a definite physical shape but this cannot be fully comprehended without the notion 'Art Deco style'.

Hence this notion is not something added in to give a fuller account but an idea without which the physical nature of the building cannot be grasped. Hence the physical and ideational features of the building are interdependent, one aspect cannot be taken in without the aid of the other. The patterns or style which comprise Art Deco can be seen as its 'logic' whilst the shapes of Art Deco buildings can be seen as the extended form of these patterns/logics.

As Godelier (1988, p.169) argues in a similar vein regarding family structure, this cannot be understood unless we see it as entailing mental categories as well as spatial relations.

> Every social relation...exists both in thought and outside of it...The mental part of a social relation consists first of all in the set of representations, principles and rules which must be 'acted upon' to engender that relation between individuals and groups...One cannot imagine individuals marrying each other without knowing what marriage is, or whilst being unaware of the kind of marriage rules operative in their society...without being acquainted with the rules of descent.

A like interdependence of the ideational and spatial occurs in the expression 'the logic of capital'. We can see this both as an immanent set of rules, the way that capital works, its rationale, and as a structure with different spaces where different processes occur (e.g. production and consumption). Both aspects seem crucial and inseparable in gaining a grasp of the characteristics of capital. Further, as with the logic of capital, 'laws of nature', combine two seemingly disparate categories - nature and logic - the one falling on the side of subjectivity and the other in the natural world. The implication of running them together, to take Farrell's point, is that thought can come to us from the outside rather than being solely a product of the subject-as-divinized-interpreter.[5]   Finally, we can take Weber's notion of ideal types as consisting in a fusion of the nomothetic (logical) and idiographic (picturing-spatial) aspects of the social world and hence as suggesting that analysis of social life depends on recognising that its entities have this dual aspect nature.

Dualism at Work: Physicalist and Cognitivist Contradictions in Foucault and Goffman

In order to gauge the plausibility of the dual aspect perspective, it will be instructive to look at the role of consciousness in explanations of agency.

Consciousness tends to either occupy a central position as with symbolic interactionists and other interpretivists, existentialist and humanist Marxists, or to be reduced to marginal status as with Foucault's view that discursive norms operate first and foremost on the body, or Butler's claim that identity is achieved via performance.

Further, sometimes a position is held (interactionist sociology, for instance) where the common sense view that ideas have influence on their own account is taken on board. This is the case with the taken for granted efficacy of labelling or stigmatising. Mind-body/subject-world dualisms however dictate that ideas belong not to the spatial world of causality and their social efficacy is rationalised along the lines that beliefs 'are real in their effects' but not real themselves. This leads to the conclusion that the effects are produced *ex nihilo*!

It will therefore be in order to examine some of the difficulties which rise from the polarised distribution of subjectivity across the subject-world divide. For example, Goffman's (1982) interactionism, although concentrating on agency as the source of social determinations, relies on an idea of the body as a pre-discursive given which connects personal and social identity through role play, impression management, institutionalisation, and so on.

Now, as Shilling (1997, pp.80-81) notes despite its importance to individual identity,

> we are left wondering how far the body is an *integral* part of human agency and not just something we are stuck with managing according to the societal norms of 'body language'...As with Foucault, the mind and how we think about the body become sites in which the meaning of the body is inscribed.

That is, societal norms (the world) are taken as the source influence of the construction/presentation of the body.

Social constructionism in the work of Foucault starts out from the opposite end of the spectrum from Goffman, in that agency is seen as produced through discourse which acts on the body through various disciplinary systems and techniques which emphasise the positioning of bodies within spatial relations such as those of the classroom or panopticon oriented prison. Here ideas or consciousness are seen as effects of the behavioural changes effected by the disciplinary processes. Ironically, Shilling (*op. cit.*, p.79) argues, the emphasis Foucault places on the constructedness of the body leads him to treat the body as a

> transhistorical and cross cultural unified phenomenon...the body is *always ready* to be constructed by discourse...the body...is a site which receives meaning from, and is constituted by external forces...On the other hand, Foucault's epistemological view of the body means that it virtually *disappears* as a material phenomenon...its existence is permanently deferred by the grids of meaning imposed by discourse...Once the body is contained within modern disciplinary systems, it is the mind which takes over as the location for discursive power. Consequently, the body tends to become an inert mass controlled by discourses centred in the mind [which is treated as if abstracted from an active human body].

What we can see from this synopsis of the disciplinary effects of discourse on the body is a kind of oscillation between cognitivism and behaviourism, through a subjectivity *sans* subject and a world without bodily locations. As Shilling (*loc. cit.*) notes, this overlooks the possibility that 'disciplinary systems of power' might be

> 'lived practices' which do not simply mark themselves on people's thoughts, but permeate, shape and seek to control their sensuous and sensory experiences.

In what follows we will investigate, independently of Shilling, how such constructions might be possible. It is however, important to note that Foucault himself saw basic, taken for granted, 'natural' categories as constructions. In *The History of Sexuality*, Foucault argues for the position that sexuality is socially constructed by discursive practices such as psychoanalysis, education or medicine. These discourses act upon the body to generate what comes to be regarded as a natural sexuality. Foucault himself, however, seems to maintain a residual naturalism of the body and its sensations (Foucault, 1979, p.168), a 'something' that precedes discourse.

As with other perspectives examined, there is a sense that bodies are, even if only notionally, as Shilling demonstrates, the base or substructure upon which discourse acts to produce ideational effects, certain belief structures. Against this it could be argued that the body is always a figure. The aesthetic sense of this is perhaps the obvious one.[6] Other illuminations of this point would include the categorisations of the body as natural, biological, erotic, which are historically specific as the Foucauldian method itself would suggest and indicate the world-subject ambiguity discussed earlier.

This 'world' character of categories reminds us of Farrell's suggestion that subjectivity should be seen principally as coming from the 'outside', rather than individual consciousness. Therefore, for Foucault to see the body as natural in the sense of preceding discourse is to fall prey to his own criticism of 'natural' categories. On the other hand, Foucault is right to sense that extradiscursive matters have a role, if we are to understand that as referring to matters beyond the cognitive sphere. The problem is then to show how there can be an outside to discourses and to do this without falling into the subject-world dualism highlighted by Shilling.

Arguably, such a project would involve taking the various discursive formations in Foucault as intersubjective rather than purely objectified forms of language practice (a 'circulation of statements'). Here, meaning is captured in the practice of language, the sense of the situation - where members' sense may differ from and contest the official sense - rather than in attempts to codify or conventionalise the practice. Hence, discursive practices of the body could be seen in the manner of action/description noted above rather than objectified description. It would then be possible to talk about the body as something which is 'done', achieved or produced without falling into the cognitivist trap as doing/describing straddles the subject-world divide. It also suggests a way out of the problem of 'labels/discourses-make-us-what-we-are', as we are already substantial in the practice of taken for granted meanings of, for example, 'the biological', 'sexual', 'natural' and so on.

An example of how the body is inscribed phenomenologically, ('described/done') is given in Garfinkel's (1967) study of Agnes. In brief, Agnes has a sex-change operation so that she can have a biological identity appropriate to her already existing sense of being a woman. The point here is that Agnes's sense of female embodiment was, Garfinkel argues, derived from having to consciously organise the performance of being a woman whereas usually the steps involved in this are hidden from the members of society and are therefore taken as 'determinants and independent objects' (*ibid.*, p.181-2). In other words, the 'observably normally sexed person' was the product of these 'inexorable' invisible processes, that is, an objectification of those processes.

> ...the commonplace recognition of normal sexuality as a 'case of the real thing' consisted of a serious, situated and prevailing accomplishment that was produced in concert with others by activities whose prevailing and ordinary success itself subjected their product to Merleau-Ponty's 'prejuge du monde' (*loc. cit.*).

The point is then that the actual (everyday) meanings of 'man and 'woman' reside in the taken for granted semantic networks of the time and place, rather than in medicalised conventions as in Foucauldian discourse (although the latter will become sedimented in the former in some way). The sense of self subjected to and confirmed in everyday life, as Merleau-Ponty's account of intersubjectivity as *L'On* in Chapter 1 makes clear, suggests something substantial, rather than either a Lacanian effect or a Sartrean isolated ego.

It is worth contrasting this position with the more recent and influential position on performance advanced by Butler (1996, p.112). Here the notion of performativity falls back into the argument that acts of naming can 'bring into being that which they name...performativity as *that aspect of discourse that has the capacity to produce what it names*...this production happens through a certain kind of repetition or recitation.'

Now the objectified meanings of those discursive practices may produce self-fulfilling processes, but arguably, this is due to the power of some to manipulate the discourse (and its Foucauldian potentialities) displacing the ability to cognise intersubjective meaning, that sense of what is going on generated in context. In other words, conversants would not be able to put a name to their sense of events. Further, they may have a different name and sense imposed through the power of institutionally-sanctioned 'repetition', etc. Friedan (1968, p.13) makes this point in relation to women's oppression which was, in the 1950s, 'the problem that has no name'. Hence naming (or its absence, substitution by other names) does not produce the kind of closure or circularity Butler intimates but rather a kind of disorientation, angst and misnaming (see Merleau-Ponty on sense in Chapter 1).[7]

The idea of an intersubjective sense of the world achieved through action in context which emerges here perhaps helps to fill out Farrell's (*op. cit.*, p.29) argument that subjectivity might be 'of the world' rather than purely in the viewpoint of the individual subject.

Now the distribution of subjectivity characterised in Farrell's (*op. cit.*, pp.249-52) account as either within the individual subject (classic modernity) or 'emptied out' individual subjectivity (poststructuralism) suggests that the dominant way of locating it is via paradigms of individualism.

In our survey of social constructionism, this conclusion is not only evident from Foucauldian-type theories of subjectivity but also in interactionist approaches. Like the Foucauldians, interactionists also employ behavioural criteria but assume that social order is constructed at a cognitive level. That is, whilst interactionism (Mead, 1970, pp.152-64) presupposes a collective idea, the generalised other, a normative standard through which behaviour is made sense of, it is deemed to operate through individual consciousnesses.

The problem with this is the asymmetry between the generalised other (idea) and individual agency (bodily dimension). That is, there is no body that corresponds to the collective idea. Consequently, an account of social construction which starts off with a shared symbolism as the embodiment of sociality ends up socially disembodied as this symbolism only appears as a product of individual minds. Hence the problem of 'other minds' (solipsism) is reproduced because individual subjectivity is not seen as configured within a social body. There is no mode of being whereby the generalised other can be shared amongst social actors. The dimension of the (intersubjective) social body (Merleau-Ponty's 'situation', for example) is missing. Similarly, in the Foucauldian case, discourse operates directly upon individual bodies; that is, individuals are not taken to have a social or cultural existence with attendant meanings through which the influence of discourse might be mediated.

As Farrell (*op. cit.*, pp.249-50) remarks of poststructuralism, there is no middle term through which meaning can be distributed (beyond agents' consciousnesses) as a feature of the world. The emphasis on an ontology of individual bodies places Foucault within the domain of the 19th century utilitarian practices he so assiduously examines.

The general conclusion to be drawn from examination of the constructionist positions is that they lack depth. That is, ideas tend to be collapsed back into individual consciousness which in turn rests on a corporeal substructure, a base which alternatively bears or produces ideational superstructure, reflections, effects. This reductionism is disabling for any attempt at giving an account of the efficacy of meaning and subjectivity as practical features of the world.

Part 2: Alternatives to Conventionalist Accounts of the Discursive

Dummett's Reading of Frege's Theory of Meaning

Dummett's conception of sense (intersubjective meaning) enables us to flesh out Farrell's proposition that thought or discourse is not merely world-as-reflected/constructed-in-the-individual-subject but is a part of the world.

In Dummett's reading of Frege's theory of meaning, a world-character is elaborated within the domain of meaning. That is, meaning is produced by the way natural language utterances are constructed out of already existing elements - phrases or names denoting an object. A kind of self-referencing goes on within these natural-discursive structures in that they both objectify their subject matter but also relate objective meanings to the context of utterance as situated meanings.

In relating the conventional senses of terms or phrases to a context of utterance a different meaning is generated - the sense of an utterance. Senses are produced *in situ* and therefore belong neither to speaker or listener but rather inhere as a common linguistic practice in the context of utterance itself. Hence such meanings are intersubjective. Further, for Dummett they are not objectified entities but 'objects of apprehension'; that is to say, they are determinate entities issuing from the way language use picks out its subject matter, the meanings produced by 'doing' language, or, arguably, any public (symbolic) display of thinking.

An example of language use as a self-referential process which evokes a sense, in this case, an awareness of an ambiguity, can be gleaned from the following joke.

> Q: What do you call a rabbit with no ears?
> A: Anything you like because it can't hear you.[8]

Here the ambiguities which lie within the taken for granted, indexical usages of 'call' facilitate the joke. In comparison, the conventional meaning narrows this down to one logical object - 'call' as in naming.

In picking something out, conventional meanings (senses) of terms are modified by their application or articulation with a context. Hence it is not the linguistic formulation used (the significance of a term or name) which gives us the sense of an utterance but the way it is employed within a context. In the case of the rabbit joke, the multiple possibilities of the context are finely poised and hence an ambiguous state of affairs is denoted. The conjunction of these two senses produces the joke utterance sense (around the ambiguity).

We can also take the joke as a metaphor for the way language utterances work in Dummett's account of natural language; that is, the process of naming objects is a self-referential process which draws on the taken for granted features of the context to modify conventional meanings.

It is worth examining in more detail what Dummett has to say about sense and its world character as it provides a way of making sense of Garfinkel's (*op. cit.*, pp.3-4) claims about the reflexivity (self-referentiality) of natural language use ('*recognizable* sense...or objectivity of accounts [are] *features* of the socially organized occasions of their use') This can be summarised in the following way. The self-referentiality of utterances can be seen in the way their descriptive, defining dimension overflows into their utterances-as-action trope, where, in the process of picking out an object, shared meaning is generated. Hence, whilst this cognitive content provides a mapping effect or framework for meaning, the actual meanings of names (terms or phrases) can only be understood via their contexts of use. That is to say, the production of meaning is overlaid by the significance or cognitive coding effects of the terms used.

The cognitive content of the individual's utterance, which is also its subjectivity, is spread over the joint linguistic activity which identifies or picks out the objects of social practices, and as a linguistic context expresses states of affairs in an indexical fashion. In so doing, the individual's utterances move beyond a mere subjectivity and take on a world character. The sense of an utterance is then the product of a process in which the subject articulates the different elements of meaning (conventional-cognitive and contextual). Thus it references itself, its subjectivity, in what it does, its linguistically-oriented (world-based) activity.

In other words, the sense of an utterance is given by the mode of relating to an object. Here, the cognitive content of the object is referenced in the common linguistic practice of picking it out, i.e. the conceptual description belongs both to the concept/name and to the utterance through which the object is identified. Dummett puts the matter thus:

> For Frege...The sense of a proper name is the way we arrive at the object, but not conceived as a means to a separable end: the apprehension of an object is not an outcome that may be detached from the process that led to it. From this standpoint, sense is better understood as the manner in which we pick out the object than as the route we take to it. We are never given an object, complete in itself; we can think about it, speak of it, or apprehend it only as presented to us in some particular way...' (*ibid.*, p.132).

Whilst the self-referentiality of the process of identifying items of discourse is evident from what Dummett says here, the situated character of the process is also made apparent. However, because some writers, Dummett argues (*loc. cit.*), have taken senses to be objectified meanings a certain kind of misunderstanding has arisen. For example, if we express the fact that we can see a building, then we must see it from a particular angle, following Frege's point about the situatedness of senses. Some have therefore concluded from the situatedness of senses that we cannot see buildings, i.e. conceptualise the whole. Dummett concludes that here the linguistic formulation, 'mode of presentation' of a matter is mistaken, detached or substituted for what it apprehends. Hence we can say then that in this case a kind of closure occurs in which literality, conventions public codes, OED definitions, etc. are taken for objects denoted in living discourse. The self-confirmatory conundrums in variants of social constructionism visited earlier in the chapter will serve as significant examples here.

As Dummett (*loc. cit.*) notes, Frege, in one strand of thinking at least, is quite clear about the separateness of senses and objects. Indeed, some senses have no objects (references), some have more than one and in other cases they have mistaken objects.

Further, whilst senses are not objects and may exist without and indeed are prior to objects/references in the way of being determined by them, for Frege the objectivity of senses is without doubt (*ibid.*, p108). They provide the bridge between the 'inner world of sense-impressions' and the 'outer world of perceptible things', that is, they link individual subjectivity with the world of public objects (*ibid.*, p.143.). For Dummett (*op. cit.*, pp.108-9, 114), shared linguistic practice and the senses thereby produced are deemed to be the real intersubjective world on which discursive objectifications are based.

As mentioned above, in picking things out, the classifying process often gets in the way of what is actually meant, denoted, in a speaker's utterance. Dummett argues this point through his distinction between senses and objects (references). How can the distinction be made in practice though? How can we break out of the world of senses into that of objects? What is to prevent an infinite regress or endless dissimulation/play of referentiality in say, the Derridean manner? Dummett's solution is to argue that all definitions, when pushed, finally fall back on context, the background or indexical features of utterances. In other words, definition finally rests on ostension; 'it is thus' (*ibid.*, pp.143-4). Ostensive definitions are themselves not infallible. For example, 'this is how you fix a bicycle puncture' may be open to disputation. However, the appeal is to the already shared implicit criteria of the context of the claim, not to an endless series of definitions.

Hence there are two aspects of referencing in the utterance. Whilst singular terms or proper names serve explicitly to pick out, or denote, objects, the background of indexical features is also involved. It operates as a mode of indirect reference; it provides a semantic context or field within which the object can be picked out. It is Dummett's (*op. cit.*, pp.47-8, 360ff) contention that these features, explicit and indirect reference, are tied together in the generative act of meaning, that is by the sense of the utterance. Explicit, denotative reference is always anchored in the referentiality of the semantic context. Hence, as Garfinkel noted, what gets denoted, objectified is always subject to a *prejuge du monde*. The corollary, as Gramsci (see Chapter 3) pointed out, is that formal knowledge is only effective insofar as it is articulated with, becomes a sediment of, common sense.

In this unity of sedimented meanings within the context of an utterance, Dummett's semantics differs sharply from semiotic theories of meaning where denotative reference is identified with significance, the formal codes used to pick things out, not the meaning context. Although connotative meanings give 'context' for Barthes, as Hall (1997, p.42) notes, this kind of context is 'static' rather than a living historical context. The consequence of this, as seen above, is that when radicalised, as in Derrida, meaning is dissimulated in search of its actuality in an endless play of difference.

Ricoeur (1986, pp.299-302) develops an (in some ways) similar view to Dummett's but which relies in the end on Husserlian transcendental reduction, the abstraction of ideal meanings from everyday activities which are then taken as the ontologically prior guiding (Platonic) framework for the latter. Ricoeur, none the less, like Dummett, identifies two sorts of reference, the conceptual-speculative and the metaphorical. However, for Ricoeur, these are not tied into a common process of meaning production but rather each has its own sense, which produces the kind of problem about getting from the inner world of the subject and its conceptualisations to public discourse that we examined above.

Importantly though, Ricoeur (*op. cit.*, p.321) also identifies the world of natural or 'ordinary' language as metaphorical, that is standing for the unspoken, indexical features of its context or semantic field.

Phenomenological Sociology as an Alternative to Conventionalism

It is now worth turning to examine how the phenomenology of language has been employed in the domain of sociology, as it may both accent the significance of Dummett's work and help to evaluate aspects of sociological phenomenology as an alternative to social constructionist theories of the conventionalist or nominalist kind mentioned earlier.

In phenomenological terms, we can draw parallels between the way utterances pick out objects and the way social interactions occur between members in the sociology of ethnomethodology. In both cases this can go ahead without theoretical grasp of what is happening, that is, it works purely on the basis of 'unattended' reflexivity, the way the background assumptions of natural language index a situation (Benson and Hughes, 1983, pp.102-3). Where processes of identifying, recognising, analysing, locating, do come into play they rest loosely on the background assumptions and can involve interpreting things according to which assumptions seem relevant at the time. Hence, however watertight definitional pronouncements may seem they are always subject to modification depending on the context in which they are applied (*ibid.*, p.109ff).

This then establishes a distinction between everyday intersubjective structures and codifying or knowledge-based theoretical language. Consequently, conventional discursive structures - rules, codes, textbook knowledge, and so on - are anchored semantically in these structures.

Ethnomethodologists would probably see themselves as a species of constructionism, and indeed, are often mentioned in the same breath as Goffman's conventionalist performativism, for example. However, Garfinkel (*op. cit.*, pp.165, 170) distances himself from Goffman's assimilation of performances - which for the former build on making sense of everyday beliefs - to theatrical performances. Ethnomethodologists make the claim that conventional sociology see its theories as reflecting reality 'out there'. Garfinkel observes (Benson and Hughes, *op. cit.*, p.103) that there is no 'time out' and that sociologists' ways of knowing about society are pervaded by a 'reflexivity of accounting practices'. In other words, the background knowledge of members, including sociologists, is a part of the world they describe: their accounts are self-referential. The inference that could be drawn from this is that the world is not real, in the sense of having depth, open-endedness because its self-referentiality implies a self-fulfilling prophecy (*ibid.*, p.102): we discover only what we have already put there. However, for ethnomethodologists, background expectations fit loosely with their codifications (*ibid.*, pp.103, 113-115), there is always an element of creative interpretation, so things never turn out fully as predicted (See Benson and Hughes' examples of applications of codes, *op. cit.*, pp.102-113). Hence, although there is a circularity around members' activities, it is not *vicious*.

Furthermore, ethnomethodologists see the background expectations as different in kind from abstract conceptual knowledge. Society or conversation is enacted though indexicality,

> coding practice, following a rule, formulating a conversation - *as examples of practical activities* - all gloss the circumstances of their production and are embedded in these circumstances (*ibid.*, p.124).

In other words, members' language does not enunciate abstract thought but occurs as a practical activity. The duality of everyday language as description/action is an underlying theme in phenomenological sociology and this sets it off from idealisations or theoretical constructions which attempt to fill the gaps in its accounts (*ibid.*, p.123).

However, two problems emerge from the ethnomethodological account of communication. One is its incipient cognitivism; self-referentiality generates synonymy between speakers, the indexing is always taken up in the way it is meant, hence the self-fulfilling nature of interactions and the perpetuation of milieux of social order; ethnomethodology consequently ignores social change. This social stasis or 'functionalist' criticism was also levelled by Heller (1984, pp.xi-xii) against Alfred Schutz, the major source of ethnomethodological ideas.

Secondly, ethnomethodology tends to dissolve the codes which members give an account of (apply) into the indexical processes themselves and this leads to the problem of what it is that orients the members' accounts of the codes, that is, of what they are acting towards. Members seem to be free to construct meaning autonomously from the formal structures for which they account. However, there must, logically, be something which has a semantic weight there to interpret. The question of the weight of formal structures and the power conferred by and through them is rarely evident in ethnomethodological studies.

The advantage of the Frege-Dummett position is by contrast twofold. Firstly, it accepts that natural language utterances are not univocal, that more that one object may be indicated, or, again, that a sense may have no corresponding objectification and therefore conversants are not necessarily talking about exactly the same things, that is producing synonymy. Secondly, the Frege-Dummett view recognises that the indexing of objects depends for its workability on idealised or abstract language (significance of the utterance) as a provider of cognitive materials, structures in the form of codes, conventions, etc. through which communicative practices can construct their actual objects, as opposed to the 'formal objects' indicated by the conventions of terminology - the dictionary definition, for example. Hence, objects are not equated with conventional classifications but the latter can act as a framework against which speakers can achieve coherence.

Consequently, whilst ethnomethodologists point out that much communication is purely indexical (has only indirect reference) the Frege-Dummett perspective would argue that this only works because the implication of reference is still there to provide coherence between conversants. That is, whilst indexical statements do not themselves identify, denote objects, the background of taken for granted ideas which is indexed can contain a fund of concepts. Hence indexical references can be traced, made explicit through examining the unexamined basis of an utterance. Indeed, this element of making sense is recognised in ethnomethodology where such tracing procedures are sometimes known as 'the documentary method' (Garfinkel. *op. cit.*, p.76ff).

Naming and Fetishism: Dummett, Ricoeur and Derrida

Now the expression of natural language's incomplete terms in explicit, propositional form is, for Dummett, only a completion of reference (denotation) in relation to what the context requires. That is, propositions do not float free from the context of their production; their references/objects can always be pushed back to the level of ostensive definition, the shared inexplicit, indexical features of the context. The meaning of a statement depends on the senses and incomplete references of the terms and phrases which make up the sentential statement. It is also conditional upon the manner of their articulation in the utterance and their relation to other propositional-type or complete references/conceptual objects picked out in the discursive practices of a culture (*ibid.*, p.461). The everyday, indexical ground cannot therefore be dispensed with, surpassed as in Hegel's conception of the development of knowledge (where everything is taken up and its truth eliminated by the proposition in the 'positive negation' of previous levels of consciousness).

The work of some 20th century writers suggests, however, that the proposition or formal statement does have a kind of autonomy and power over its grounds - which are in any case seen as superseded by it. Weber's work on rationalisation, Foucault's notion of discourse as the circulation of statements, the recitation and repetition of Butler's (*op. cit.*, p.112) naming procedures (following Foucault, Austin and Derrida) are key examples in the literature, but Dummett (pp.110, 132ff, 459-60) also notes the tendency of writers working in epistemology and language, such as Davidson, Kripke and McDowell to mistake significance (what are referred to here as 'formal objects') for sense, and indeed reference.

The incompleteness of indexical features of utterances and their polyvalence regarding determinate meanings - senses without references - marks them out as different in kind from propositional-type language. In Husserl's terms, they represent an open horizon for the construction of similar representations - whatever is deemed to make sense within the context and hence in Schutz's (*op. cit.*, p.7) appropriation of Husserl, an 'open horizon of typical familiarity'.

The question of why there should be a general tendency towards substitution of significance or abstract categories for actual meanings can be related back to the rationalising and reifying tendencies of the institutional structures of modern bureaucratic capitalist societies. Here perhaps both in Adorno's (1973) sense of closed or self-identical subjectivity and Foucault's insistence on the power of institutions to circulate statements, or again, the notion of repetition, or Derrida's (1974) *usure*, the wearing away of metaphorical richness - all signifying the power to displace other meanings - must surely be crucial insights here.

Perhaps most of the implications here can be captured in Derrida's (Ricoeur, *op. cit.*, pp.285-6) account of worn-away metaphor. The passage of meanings into silence through familiarity of usage at the same time objectifies or conventionalises them. They become senses with (misplaced) conventional references.

Hence, the actual meanings then work outside the consciousness of speakers. For Derrida, this is a kind of surplus value, an excess of meaning, a sediment or trace whose silence renders the conventional meaning fetishistic. In the labour of the production of meaning, the metaphorical surplus is denied to the speaker and only becomes visible in the autonomous functioning of language. Furthermore, worn-away metaphor is taken for pure (abstract) conceptual thought, an idealisation or abstraction from the living language, although in reality, it hides that within it.

Marx's (1974, pp.76-7) comments on fetishism suggest a form of suturing via the *social* relations of capitalism in which the individual is separated from its products. Whilst Derrida prefers a *linguistic* explanation, the broader account may rest with Marx.

This examination of conventional meaning has implications for ethnomethodological studies for, as we have seen, a great deal of ingenuity is involved in everyday, indexical linguistic functioning. However, the codes and conventions of which members give accounts, themselves seem to replace the extra-discursive realists' domain of the 'out-there'. That is, no explanation of the dynamic relationship between propositional language and its indexical context is given.

However, Dummett (*op. cit.*, p.461) offers some light on this matter when he observes that the proper or denotative reference of a statement is determined in accordance with the indexical features of the context of an utterance. That is, its object is dependent on the way the speaker grasps the references/senses of its constituent parts, that is, the way they are articulated within the context - which establishes therefore via its sedimented meanings what sort of truth value it expresses. For example, the articulation of conservatism within its discursive tradition produced different meanings in the 1950s and '60s from those of the 1980s. In this sense 'Everyday life is the measure of all things'.[9] The emergence of reference from the context of the utterance is then a key element of the

Frege-Dummett perspective and one which is overlooked by those who substitute significance (codified meaning, conventions) for sense.[10]

In Ricoeur's (*op. cit.*, p.299) characterisation of this emergence, the metaphorical character of natural language enables speaker's utterances to become a focus of different and shifting fields of reference which facilitate the picking out of differing objects. Both Kuhn (1970) and Lakatos (1972) have via 'paradigm shifts' and 'problemshifts' referred to processes which resemble this. In Chapter 1, the evolution of the Sony Walkman conventionally designated a mobile cassette player with headphones and shared listening device but which only made sense in the context of mobile, personal listening was given as an example of how users entered and switched semantic fields, generating new identities for the Walkman. The semantic networks of its genealogy provided the raw materials for metaphorising, actualising ('it's like this') and identifying the Walkman.

Finally, this picking out-as-doing trope of reference inscribes materiality in communicative practice: for Dummett, the world of common linguistic practices must ultimately be the real world of making sense and attempts to ground discursive materiality in the physicality of the body rather than in a *sense* of embodiment will, paradoxically, as Garfinkel shows, only serve to dematerialise the body!

Notes

[1]   Hence the Hegelian or, more strictly, Spinozist view, that ideas categoriality are a feature of things is followed in this discussion.

[2]   Rather than subjectivising the world, Farrell (*op. cit.*, pp.221-2) argues that patterns or logics discerned in it are part of a process of self-relating in which we discover the objectivity of reason.

[3]   The 'currant bun' metaphor can be seen to carry over into discourse theory too, where subjects become 'bearers' of discursive positions. As McNay (1994, pp.76-7) points out, Foucault's subject positions fail to engage with the actuality of individual subjectivity, for example, how prediscursive identities like 'woman' affect an individual's ability to occupy a discursive subject position.

[4]   Bodily posture or 'body language' can be used to illustrate the claim that an ideational supplement exists in our sense of the physical.

[5]   The idea of understanding emphasised in this Chapter and throughout is that of a practical accomplishment and is akin to that mentioned by Wittgenstein (cited in Chapter 2) in the sense that processes of understanding are seen as taking place in the public, spatially-extended world rather than in the mind, conceived as the private realm of thoughts.

[6]   See also Note 4 above.

[7]   Whilst the power of institutional identities to impose their meanings clearly requires their sedimentation within the everyday and, as Hull (1997, p.24) notes in her

comparison of Adorno and Butler on identity, indicates their materiality, it does not exhaust identity. For Adorno, this means the subject rather than being identical with the claims of discourse may experience a 'tangible misery'. It is a denial that discourse is itself mediated by what it mediates.

[8] I am grateful to my daughter, Katharine, for providing this illustration of the relationship between naming and reference.

[9] Guy Debord cited in Osborne (1995, p.192).

[10] Dummett's (*op. cit.*, p.134) point that senses can have more than one reference and that indexical accounts facilitate this process illustrates the peculiar nature of indexicals or contextual meaning. It is both determinate in its articulation in different contexts and yet undifferentiated from the point of view of theoretical knowledge. The role of cultural studies can be delineated here as picking out the 'undifferentiated' differentiations occurring and contesting in semantic fields yet articulated in everyday language and new cultural meanings emerge.

7 Space, Time and the Everyday: Jameson and Osborne

Recent years have seen a renewed interest in the meaning of space and time and of their relative importance. The traditional dominance of time over space has been contested by postmodern writers. The significance of spatial metaphors in accounting for the meaning of the culture of modern capitalism has displaced a traditional concern with its temporal unfolding, indeed, on one account (Fukyama, 1992) history itself may have come to an end.

Nonetheless, writers like Jameson have expressed an on-going concern about temporality through the theme of a mediatised culture which erases historicity. In many ways Jameson continues the pessimism of the Frankfurt School, who themselves emphasised the distortional and manipulative aspects of popular cultural forms. In his (1991) analysis of postmodern culture, space itself provides a figure for grasping a textuality without referents or fixed meanings, a surface without depth and a concomitant ideological closure within signifying systems.

On the other hand, Osborne (1995) has focussed on the configurations of temporality and the need to see these as both related to experience and as an independent register of historical development. The emancipatory aim to grasp historical trends requires an awareness of the openness of the future, but this is only to be achieved by contesting the dominant conception of history which through a 'politics of time' effects a temporal closure.

In the following account, the concerns about a media-oriented culture which has manipulative and distortional effects in contemporary capitalist societies are examined in the light of a practice-oriented view which distinguishes the context of utterance and reading, the sense of the communication from the conventions or codes through which it is expressed.

Fredric Jameson: The Semiotics of 'Late Capitalism'[1]

Jameson's (1991) analysis of the 'cultural logic of late capitalism' uses Barthes' semiotics to argue that texts now reference each other rather than the world; that language has been separated from the world. Further, the dominant, denotative meanings have been undermined by the play of signs/signifiers. The modernist models of inner/outer, essence and appearance, authenticity/inauthenticity give way to a new affectivity which diffuses through surfaces rather than depths (*ibid.*, p.12). However, this transformation is itself a historical matter and thus points beyond the text to that which organises it.

Hence, Jameson wishes to keep some elements of the modernist scheme. These further include some sense that denotation still has a function, since for signs:

> we observe that in their moment of intersection a new hierarchy is at once established in which one sign becomes something like the material on which the other one works, or in which the first sign establishes a content and a center to which the second is annexed for auxiliary and subordinate functions...

although these can change places rapidly and ceaselessly, as witnessed in the development of promo video techniques (*ibid.*, p.87). The seemingly arbitrary juxtapostioning of images in promo videos in fact only make sense if we treat them not as isolated signs but as a narrative structure, that is as discourse rather than a semiotic event standing on its own (*ibid.*, p.86).

Now in the first Barthes schema, the semiotics of *Mythologies*, the literal meaning of a sign stands in a connotative relation to other signs. The peculiarity of this relationship is that the literal or denotative reference is transformed by this relationship into something other than 'objective' language.[2] The connotative elements act back on the denotation producing a second order meaning in which the denotative sign replaces what it signifies as the reality of the text. Barthes describes, through advertisements and other striking images, everyday contexts in which this process occurs. This metaphorical mode has also been described by Empson (1985, pp.4-5), who argues that the force of metaphor is derived from the way metaphorical contrast or comparisons react on the 'topic' or cognitive language, producing affective associations, and so in the use of language, the cognitive element is never completely separate.

Barthes' famous example of the process of generating myths is the *Paris Match* picture of the black French soldier saluting the flag. Whilst on the surface this is a picture of a soldier demonstrating loyalty, the connotations on which its mythical/metaphorical meaning depends include the legitimacy of French colonialism.

The standpoint from which Barthes (1972) addresses myth is that of demystification, of ideological critique. For this reason, the early Barthes (and presumably Jameson, but see below) comes in for criticism from, for example, Silverman and Torode (1980, pp.265-6), for taking a position outside the meaning process as the unsituated, absolute, divinized commentator. Now whilst the images Barthes analyses for ideological content must be expressed propositionally in order to extract invalid truth claims, the fact of the matter is that this is seldom the way images are expressed. It has been argued in previous chapters that everyday language must be seen in terms of its use rather than as a cryptic epistemology. We can only understand it if we can grasp the context of utterance. Here understanding involves seeing what the language does, grasping its performative meaning. This, to unpack what has been argued above, necessitates distinguishing conventional meaning from the reference denoted by the context of the utterance. This does not entail any epistemological God's eye view, but to understand in the same way as the participants in a conversation understand. Whilst Barthes describes myth as part truth and part ideology, the Frege-Dummett perspective focuses on the senses expressed by utterances through which contextual meaning can be read or denoted in the topic.

The significance of this discussion for Jameson, is that whilst he wishes to reject the early Barthes's ideology critique as positing a knowable world out-there, an absolute standard against which to judge ideology, he also wishes to retain a notion of ideology compatible with Barthes' later work on intertextuality in which the out-there functions as a residual reminder of the distortional effects of ideology but whose complexity defies orthodox modes of reference.[3] Here Barthes (Barthes, 1975 for example) argues that meaning is not oriented towards literality or the referent but, on the contrary, that texts exist in a constant play of self-referentiality-registering each others' meanings as connotative frameworks for their own. A further twist of this development from Jameson (*op. cit.*, p.84) is that in, for example, video texts such as promo videos, ideology is already reconstructing denotation (conventional meaning) through insertion of connotations within the 'literal' itself.

Barthes originally assigned 'authenticity to the denotative value of the photographic image' which is then undermined where 'advertising texts take that original denotative text as their own new content'. Here existing images work in 'the service of some heightened play of degraded thoughts and commercial messages' (*loc. cit.*). However, it is always possible to point to the authentic primary text as a means of demystification. In the new circumstances of the intertextual play of terms, images and so on, represented, for example, by video text, this is no longer possible as 'the ideological signs are already deeply embedded in the primary texts'. A further complication is that topic and theme, subject and predicate now rapidly interchange in the above mentioned process of 'distraction'. Here Jameson gives the example of the development of logos from the earlier sign, the brand name which starts off as denotator of jeans or shirts, for example.

Within the context of promo videos, this situation is transformed and the real world as referent disappears altogether. The brand name-as-logo becomes a denotator in its own right; as 'synthesis of advertising image and brand name', even embodying a whole advertising tradition (*ibid.*, p.85). The logo must be possessed for its own sake and can go on to reference other subordinate items such as jeans or shirts. Similarly, in the video film *AlienNATION* (*ibid.*, p.93) the symbolism of a milk carton with a bullet hole could reference an historical event, or, alternatively the historical event (assassination of Harvey Milk) could denote the bullet-holed milk carton.[4] In the same video Beethoven's music is contextualised and degraded by the connotator 'classical music', which operates like the logo in relation to the brand name. For Jameson this trope represents a kind of ideological closure in which the real world referent is effaced. The process of reification of the signifier represented in Barthes' notion of myth disjoins the sign from the referent. However, at first:

> Such a disjunction does not completely abolish the referent, or the objective world, or reality which still continue to entertain a feeble existence on the horizon like a shrunken star...But its great distance from the sign now allows the latter to enter a moment of autonomy...This autonomy of culture...is the moment of modernism...of a realm of the aesthetic which redoubles the world...winning a certain negative or critical power (*ibid.*, p.96).

However, the postmodern phase where 'reification penetrates the sign itself' means that:

reference and reality disappear altogether...We are left with a pure and random play of signifiers...which no longer produces monumental works of the modernist type but ceaselessly shuffles the fragments of preexistent texts...metatexts which collate bits of other texts - such is the logic of postmodernism (*ibid.*, p.96).

Semiotics and the Problem of Closure

As seen above, the two connected linguistic characteristics of closure noted by Jameson are a tendency towards self-referentiality and the invasion of the sign by ideological connotators. This predicament is reinforced by Jameson's scene-setting of referent versus culture, language versus reality, and at another level, global capital as hidden or noumenal instigator of cultural changes - the base-superstructure configuration with a vengeance.

The plausibility of the closure scenario depicted by Jameson will now be examined under two of his key categories, those of ideology and semiotics.

(a) Ideology

Although Jameson's use of 'ideology' differs from the traditional Marxist view in that it has given up on reflecting reality, there is still an indecipherable causal relation with late capitalism. Moreover, there is also the problem of truth: ideology remains a matter for epistemological treatment.

Now it was argued in Chapter 4 that the base-superstructure model is better replaced by the structure in dominance/structure of structures model where the economy functions both through itself and through its interconnections with other institutions. Hence the broad 'surface' of cultural practices become conditions of production and there is no noumenal or hidden structuring of, in this case, late twentieth century societies.

Following from this perspective, ideology is not an abstraction or set of detached meanings floating in a platonic realm which reflect, or reflect only enigmatically, economic relations but is a practised part of everyday life. Ideology as a field of connotations is therefore significant not so much for what it says, but as for what it does. In the tradition of Gramsci and Althusser ideology creates a subjective content for people, it also shapes institutional structures - 'creates the terrain on which men move, struggle, acquire consciousness of their position etc.', in Gramsci's words.

It was argued in Chapters 3 and 4 that there is an overlap between this perspective and the phenomenological work of writers such as Husserl, Schutz, Garfinkel, Russell and the Frege-Dummett position. This is perhaps most usefully elaborated by Dummett (1981). For our purposes here the key point, apart from the perception of language as practice, is that discourse is functionally differentiated in terms of sense and denotative reference although such functions remain interdependent. It is important to note here that the denotative in Barthes refers to what Dummett means by 'significance', the coding procedures of a language. On the other hand, to denote, for Dummett is to pick out something as a topic in a discussion, which is grasped via the sense of the interchange, its meaning in context. There is here an idea that meaning and language are not statically related, or that meaning can be reduced to a language which ignores the contextual practices of picking things out. This distinction and deficiency in Barthes translates to Jameson's cultural analysis.

(b) Semiotics

The crucial distinguishing feature of the Frege-Dummett approach is that meaning occurs *through* language functions rather than *purely in* them. Language and actions are bound together as utterances without a reduction occurring either way.

Now whilst 'objective', conventional meanings as in Barthes' 'denotation' might indicate a certain linguistic or cultural self-sufficiency, senses, the use of language to pick out a topic, point to the openness of natural language utterances to context. Now semiotics might suggest a similar contextuality in that meaning is derived from a field of reference or connotation, the present to a speaker or reader. The difference is, of course, that the sense is expressed through the contextual usage, not the internal semiotic structure of meaning. Jakobson's observation (cf. Chapter 4), taken as representative here, that the meaning of a term is that of the term which is substituted for it illustrates this contrast well enough.

Semiotics therefore rests largely on synonymy as the measure of the relationship between terms whereas for the Frege-Dummett perspective context rather than synonymy is the key to the meaning of utterances.

Symbols, terms, phrases or sentences can have an equivalence in Frege's theory of sense and reference.[5] Different names or sentences can carry the same meaning or sense and the same name or sentences can carry different meanings. Hence there is no one-to-one relationship between sense and reference in Frege. The logical objects as conventional meanings 'denoted' by the utterance may be quite different from the sense of the utterance - our appreciation of what it would take to show the truth of the utterance in a given context and therefore the actual thing denoted. Hence, while the morning star and the evening star denote the same logical object, the senses attached to those names are not the same and can only be grasped by reference to the discourses containing those terms.

Similarly, Dummett (*op. cit.*, pp.340-2, 493) argues that attempts at translation of natural languages based purely on synonymy will fail because they do not take into account the point that the transparency of the internal structure of discourse to conversants depends on their grasping the indexical features through which one statement or expression comes to imply another. In other words, the unfolding of discourse depends on a logic of implication which is not self-evidently available from the words themselves. Rather, taking the point made (judgment) in a statement depends on grasping the context of the utterance, through which it becomes clear how the parts of the statement are related to each other, that is, how they implicate each other. An illustration of how this works can be given from the following sentence which represents a case of ambiguity in natural language: 'Wright kicked the ball, the referee blew his whistle and it went wide.' Without some contextual knowledge of the meaning of 'it went wide', for example, it is not clear that the latter is the predicate for the name/subject 'Wright kicked the ball'. Another case is mentioned by Greimas (1983) in Schleifer (1987, pp. 76-7). Here the construction of a joke depends on the meaning of 'toilette'. The word is introduced into a context as 'lovely toilettes' where it literally makes no sense as it is already a part of the context (indexical features) of the conversation, as its other meaning, 'smart occasion' and is therefore read as 'lovely lavatories'. Consequently, a translation based on synonymy would make no sense. The statement only becomes comprehensible once we detect the incorrect usage of 'toilettes'. This is not however given by the other terms in the conversation but by the context (indexicality) in which the conversation occurs. Greimas (Schleifer, *loc. cit.*) argues in his *Structural Semantics* that the 'sense' of a discourse rarely depends on synonymy (although it provides a necessary foil in the same way as conventional meaning or significance generally provides an identity *against* which denotation identifies) but on shared or 'redundant' meanings given by and constitutive of the context.

The existence of redundant or taken for granted meanings should alert us to de-reifying tendencies in discursive practices where conventional meanings are modified or subverted by the indexical features of context.

Sense and Referent

It is evident from Jameson's discussion of Barthes' semiotics that he rejects attempts to site the stability of meaning in the Saussure-Hjelmsev-early Barthes tradition of denotation. Saussure, for example, tied signified and signifier together via the metaphor that they were like the opposite sides of a sheet of paper, which if cut from one side would have immediate effects for the other.

Jameson also dismisses the possibility of anchoring meaning in a referent. Whilst the problems of correspondence theories of meaning and truth have also been rehearsed in Chapter 5, it is however worth examining what Jameson has to say on this subject. He observes that:

> at an outer limit, the sense people have of themselves and their own moment of history may ultimately have nothing whatsoever to do with its reality: that the existential may be absolutely distinct, as some ultimate 'false consciousness' from the structural and social significance of a collective phenomenon (*ibid.*, pp.281-2).

This can be immediately contrasted with the Frege-Dummett perspective where the senses of discursive expressions point beyond them and in doing so make ontological claims for meaning structures which are seated in everyday communication, that is, in the indexical expressions of natural language utterances. Here language is seen as a practice where action and description are combined, the doing and describing are two sides of the same coin - an action which describes and a description which is communicatively efficacious. It was argued in Chapter 4 that there were important similarities between this view and the work on ideology in Gramsci, Althusser and Laclau. That everyday, ideological, symbolic systems were important for what they brought about rather than as a field of mistaken truth claims. At the same time, this meant that everyday language and imagery was tied up with objective, propositional language and that translations could be made from one to the other. The notion of articulation in Gramsci was particularly suggestive in this respect, indicating a point of intersection between these aspects of language which both enlivens objective language and ties it into the everyday. Similarly, on the Frege-Dummett view, the utterance of objective language, the process of denotative reference, depends on indexical features given by the context of utterance, those elements which are transparent between speakers. Garfinkel's (1967, p.4) observation about the necessarily incomplete nature of any substitution of objective terms for indexical features of utterances is apt here.

This broad area of agreement about the dependence of cognitive language, knowledge statements on everyday contextualisation stands in contrast to Jameson's own position, which is itself, arguably, a caricature of the classical Marxist notion of ideology. Marx (1974, p.29) himself allowed for a kernel of knowledge within the shell of ideology.

The idea that there is no point of connection, no overlapping logic between the structural and collective aspects of the world and the mediatised culture whose ubiquity Jameson wishes to emphasise, would seem on the face of it to be an idealist separation of the world of experience from the world of structures, global economics and so forth. Frege (Carl, 1994, pp.63-6) warns it is a mistake to view our concepts as disembodied entities and to take the syntax of communication for its content. The subject-predicate formulation suggests that concepts exist in isolation from the factors that condition them. He is at pains to point out that in fact concepts always exist in relation to their conditions of possibility, the conditions of the utterance of statements in the Frege-Dummett view.

Frege's point about the organic connection between subject and predicate, the *actuality* of the conceptual or theoretical, helps to demonstrate the power of articulation on a larger scale, the ability to enliven an idea by tapping into the historical sense of a tradition/project à la Merleau-Ponty (see Chapter 1). It is perhaps in the light of this ontology of meaning that Jameson's (*op. cit.*, pp.21-5) claims about the waning of historical referents/reference should be viewed.

Jameson entertains the possibility of writing a fiction whose 'historical' characters only *formally* represent historical events; that is, a fiction in which the names of historical figures are utilised as divorced from their historical resonances.

Developing the theme more generally, Jameson notes:

> there no longer does seem to be any organic relationship between the American history we learn from school books and the lived experience of the current multi-national, high-rise, stagflated city of the newspapers and of our own everyday life (*ibid.*, p.27).

One argument against this dehistoricisation of symbols is that which follows on from the position developed above. This is Gramsci's insistence (cf. Chapter 3) that the historical culture is there, locked up and articulated within the 'cultural us', and that it does not depend on 'individuated consciousnesses'. The culture is something that we intersubjectively practice, whether or not it reaches the level of our consciousness. Furthermore, Jameson's emphasis on *mediatised* culture translates to the margins the more mundane but pervasive aspects of everyday life such as juridical and political structures, educational and familial practices, the ecology of the urban environment and the interconnections between all of these things.

The Historical Referent: From Jameson to Gramsci

The concern with a referent, a reality out-there is, as suggested in Chapter 6 and above, a misconception of the real, which ignores the contribution of the subjective to the world. As Farrell notes of Hegel:

> the logical structure of thought seems to be present...wherever there is any kind of self-unifying or self-determining going on [mind-independent, real processes]. So when the strong realist claims that reality articulates itself into units and sorts, even apart from how humans think, it seems that Hegel would see such a realist as granting the presence of thought in the world, in the very way in which things are determinate (Farrell, 1994, pp.16-17).

That is, the world itself is patterned, regular and intelligible; it has a logic of its own.

If this is taken on board, the effacement of the referent as posed by Jameson, can be seen as a pseudo-problem. This is so not because there are no referents but is due rather to referents not having the 'out-there' quality attributed to them by Jameson and others who maintain a simple 'subject-object' perspective.

Again, as Dummett (*op. cit.*, pp.58-9) argues, Frege's realism consists in regarding senses of expressions as having an objective status, indeed a status which determines reference (objectification). When we grasp the sense of an expression, we have an appreciation of the conditions which would render it true. We understand the way it relates to or articulates with other expressions. We can conduct conversations and thus have shared understandings (*ibid.*, p.394) about how to apply truth conditions - what it would take for a claim to be true. Thus, sense determines reference; we pick out aspects of the world through our actions and are consequently able to give cognitive accounts of them.

Articulating the Past

Now if this is seen in relation to Gramsci's notion of articulation (cf. Chapter 3), then we can understand the past precisely in the way it is articulated in the present. Current articulations of traditions of thought such as liberalism secure a hegemonic culture by drawing on the 'inarticulate' context of the tradition to contest the accounts of the historical present given by other traditions.

The reality of the past, as Gramsci indicates, remains a graspable reality not merely because it once happened but because it is bound up in present practices and can be brought to consciousness through a process of articulation with explicit ideas or theories about the past. Hence Jameson's concern with the historical referent 'out-there' has led him to neglect the referent as continually re-enacted in the culture in its more or less conscious articulations with historical presents.

The notion of articulation in Gramsci is spelled out by Hall (1986) when he (Hall) discusses the nature of political practices. Ideological frameworks take off politically if they can become organic, that is, connect with the sedimented past practices of the culture effectively.

For Gramsci, Hall (*op. cit.*, xii-xiii) argues, the locus of such historical sedimentation is common sense political thinking which:

> is composed of the historical traces, incomplete borrowings, diluted concepts and prejudices, inherited wisdoms and formulations incorporated from a variety of the 'great systems' of political thought which have sedimented into it.

Further,

> Logically and philosophically elaborated thought leaves its traces in...everyday common sense. Conversely, the pattern of common sense beliefs sometimes achieves a more rigorous...philosophical elaboration...He [also] argued that the centre of attention must be those ideologies which have influenced the thought and action of the great mass of the people...which help to form mass consciousness and provide the ideas commonly in use and categories in which apparently spontaneous practical thought generally occurs. Such ideologies, he argued had achieved true

historical or 'organic' influence...political ideas 'become organic' by being absorbed into the structure of common sense and common practice.

In Dummett's (*op. cit.*, p.461) case, the meanings of the constituent phrases or terms of an utterance constitute a sedimentation of meaning in relation to the present utterance; that is, their meanings become organic to the present utterance which both supersedes and rearticulates these meanings around a new sense and topic. The senses of the constituents are not determined by the whole utterance, its conventional meaning is different from the effective meaning which is produced by the way the constituents are configured or articulated in the sentential utterance, that is, as 'corresponding to its structure'. Therefore the whole utterance makes sense by articulating its subordinate elements, by rendering them contextual and inarticulate.

Consequently, articulation as 'making sense' involves rendering the senses of constituent phrases consonant with that of the utterance. It makes the past applications of expressions or phrases congruent with present applications, demonstrates the connections between explicit, propositional-type language and the inarticulate, indexical context of meaning, the sedimented meaning that the present utterance comes to define. In turn, the sedimented context of the utterance renders the latter obvious, ostensibly true or self-evident (*ibid.*, pp.339-41).[6] For example, in the historical context of Locke's *Treatise on Civil Government*, it made sense to define individual freedom both in terms of property ownership and of the production of property by one's own agency, and generally within the tradition of liberalism the connection between life, liberty and property became self-evident.

The configuration of clusters of meanings to produce self-evident claims is a theme of Husserl's work on sedimentation. Whereas Hall notes of Gramsci that cultural meaning requires an articulation of the (ideological) elements, Husserl makes a point about the reactivation of sediments configured as a combination. The original meaning can only be conveyed where all the members of the combination operate as a configuration (Husserl, 1970, pp.361-2). If only the individual members are reactivated then 'the ontic validity is destroyed' (*ibid.*, p.362).[7] Where the associative connections of significations work without self-evidence it is not possible to elaborate effective meaning structures. Merleau-Ponty (see Chapter 1) has made a related point about historical projects coming to an end state where they no longer connect to the demands of the situation, become 'non-sense'.

Hall's (1986a) reading of Thatcherism is pertinent here (cf. Chapter 4). He points out that the ideology is intrinsically unstable. It is connotatively problematic in that the unity of the combination of ideological elements is dependent on the figure of Thatcher rather than being founded in their mutual association. In other words, the ideology does not have a thoroughly cohesive structure, there is no cultural resonance which would have rendered it generally organic. For example, whilst the figure of Thatcher connotes both individual entrepreneurial initiative *and* family values, the connections between these ideological elements are not *culturally* self-evident.

The Historical Past as Sediment[8]

In the discussion of Gramsci and the Frege-Dummett perspective, we have elucidated the idea that articulation and its self-evidencing features provide a way of talking about the relation of past to present times. It provides a way of understanding Jameson's 'cultural dominant', which is a dominant discourse in the sense that any elaborated account of culture would occur through it and because references to previous times would form a sedimented, indexical context or framework to the exposition of current more or less conscious cultural conventions such as political programmes, economic theories, aesthetics, forms of popular culture, and so on. That is, although the cultures of other temporalities may be spoken about, *their presence within the current dominant discourse* is below the horizon of consciousness as its contextual self-evidential features.

However, in Jameson's approach it was found that cultural signifiers equivalenced each other, or 'swallowed each other up', semantically. Hence, his predominantly semiotic approach suggests the self-referentiality of signifiers which leaves no remainder, no sedimented, open horizon of meanings. In this respect one is reminded of the criticism of Hegel's idea of negation as an area (of closure) where thought is identical with itself. Indeed, this reservation was the substance of the Gadamerian fusion of horizons, as Warnke (*op. cit.*, p.165) argued, in that it represented a 'deabsolutised' form of negation, within which dialogue and difference/disagreement were still possible.

The argument had been put in its most devastating form by the young Hegelian, Feuerbach, writing in the 1840s. Feuerbach noted that any transcending account of an existing argued position must 'paradoxically' take note of the reality of that position in order to address it and supersede it. However, the reality in the first position, rather than being considered as dialogically on-going with the second, is somehow absolutely negated, or in Dews's (1986, p.38) terms becomes 'the waste product of identity thinking'. Feuerbach (1987, pp.95-6) went on to argue that the past is never 'over' in the sense described here, but lives on and co-exists with that which supersedes it. Hence Hegel's system 'knows only subordination and succession; co-ordination and succession are unknown to it'; the fact that stages in change and development form 'moments in a simultaneous totality of nature' is ignored.

If this schema is translated into the context of the preceding discussion of articulation then we can understand the self-evidential context of the cultural dominant as that which situates dominant conventional meanings of a culture and in some sense co-exists with it as 'present past'. Further, the co-existent past of a culture, as Dummett makes clear in his distinction between sense and conventional meaning, has the capacity to subvert the objectified, received meanings of the culture.

Althusser and the Conjunctural Formulation of Historical Moments

Following on from Feuerbach's suggestion about the possibility of grasping history not as a reflection of the discourses of the present but as 'simultaneous totality', it is worth investigating one celebrated project in this direction. Althusser's (1975, 1977) model of structural overdetermination was applied to the articulation question, in posing the problem of whether it was possible to get an overview of the different rhythms, paces of development and historical times as a conjuncture rather than as disparate and disjunctive processes.

Althusser argued that it was possible to describe historical trends by taking an 'essential section' or snapshot which showed how all the separate elements were both functionally and contradictorily related. However, as Osborne (1992, pp.82-3) has pointed out, the effect of this is to lose the sense of historical dynamism, change, in which one can theorise 'the break', the moment of systemic rupture which is so central to Althusser's account of overdetermination. That is, totalisation occurs not abstractly but from a particular historical situation or standpoint in relation to which all other times are understood and culminate as historical movement.

Arguably, the difficulty here in accounting for discursive-structural relations lies in the theoretical underdevelopment of the structuralist paradigm itself. The terms or elements of the conjuncture are framed in terms of the binary tropes of opposition/equivalence. Hence the problem of how one might relate or articulate temporally differentiated discursive structures, which was rehearsed in relation to Jameson, also surfaces here. There is a lack of the internally-related functions in naming or signifying and contextual indexicality which can account for the sedimentation of the past within the present.

This stands in contrast to the historical-linguistic reading of articulation outlined above which allows for a differentiation of functions. As context, the sedimented meaning is qualitatively different in character from the cultural dominant through which it achieves conscious expression. This can be seen in Gramsci's concern with rendering political programmes organic, connecting them with the relatively stable but open horizon of sedimented ideas and practices.

Further, whilst Althusser's 'essential section' suggests the historical investigator has a God's-eye view of the conjuncture and hence must stand beyond the historical process itself, it is clear that all observers are historically situated and therefore must stand in one of the temporalities of the conjuncture.

If this is the case, then understanding can arguably come from the process of articulation of the different temporalities from the standpoint of one of them. This raises the possibility of a Gadamerian fusion of horizons or a rearticulation of the elements in the Gramscian sense, where a problem can only be addressed by recognising that historical change requires that it is addressed and reformulated through a new field of connotations. In either case, the outcome is seen as a broadening of understanding, in Gramsci's case because new articulations must take account of progressive cycles of sedimentation.

The dialogical potentialities of the Gramscian perspective, as developed here, therefore seem to offer more scope for historical understanding than the pure synchrony of structuralism. The process of articulation as active sedimentation of alternative positions within one's own discourse as its programmatically inflected common sense features in some ways reflects Hegel's *Aufhebung* (transcendence) but leaves the semi-autonomous or open character of common sense intact, allowing for the possibility voiced by Gramsci that hegemony over the sediments can be contested and the everyday mobilised for another purpose.

Capitalism, Modernity and the Significance of Remembering

Jameson's pessimism for the possibility of remembering the past seems to owe something to Benjamin's (1985, p.35) work on time and commodification. One of the central ideas here is that of fashion. Fashion is a constitutive feature of our time-consciousness. Styles, forms of sensibility, discourse undergo rapid and periodic change which leaves a sense of historical dislocation. Osborne (1995, p.140) has argued that the phenomenon of dislocation has to do with the standardisation of time in the modern period. That is, 'the present' is punctuated by periodic interruptions as a kind of repetition or bureaucratisation of change. Any dislocation is hence itself routinised as repetition - the words 'fashion' and 'vogue' indicate the serial and routine nature of the apprehension of change in modernity. The routinisation of dislocation is also connected with the resistance of consciousness to shock, as noted in Simmel and Benjamin. That is, the continuity of historical events and processes is suppressed in a distancing adjustment through which the individual damps down their immediacy, a kind of abreactiveness to the bad side of things. This distancing trope is objectified in the collective temporalisation of events, 'that was then, this is now'.

For Benjamin and Osborne, this mechanism can also be seen as a commodification of time which places 'other' times beyond our grasp. The most concrete expression of this tendency for us today is perhaps the heritage industry, but the notion of history as heritage was one with which Benjamin was already familiar (*loc. cit.*).

Benjamin argues that time can only be redeemed through a quasi-theological strategy of positing a beyond to history from which point time recoalesces into a historically intelligible form. This is to be achieved by relating an image which dislocates the historical present both to the latter's everydayness and to narrative structures through which the continuity of historical processes is expressed. Thus, the everyday is reunited with narrative historical understanding (*ibid.*, pp.143-53).

Osborne (*op. cit.*, pp.189-96) also gives a reading of Lefebvre's (1971, 1987, 1991) account of the everyday which points up the contradictoriness of the everyday and its relation to standardised, commodified time. Whilst the everyday, taken for granted mode of understanding has no boundaries and is projected into an endless present in the form of cycles of repetition or in Heller's (1984) terms 'repetitive praxis', this process is affected by commodification, as capitalism itself moves in cycles of expanded reproduction, repetition or renovation of previous stages. Consequently, phenomenological experience of the new in modernity takes the form 'more of the same', 'we've seen it all before' etc.; or, as Osborne cites Heidegger 'In everydayness everything is all one and the same, but whatever the day may bring is taken as diversification' (*ibid.*, p.194). Hence, whilst the everyday is the site of repetition, these changes or repetitions in the times of capitalism conflict with the open horizons of sedimented practice where there are no objectifying boundaries. Lefebvre, in fact, relates this contradiction within everydayness to the advent of the differentiation of institutions concomitant with modern capitalism which produce objectified, specialised forms of knowledge. By contrast, in the premodern period thought was more strongly characterised by its indexical features, a transparency in its appeals to a traditional authority that, so to speak, 'always is', in its positioning within endless *calendrical* cycles.

It is in order to return at this point to Jameson's 'loss of the referent' theme, because it is precisely this phenomenology of the everyday that Jameson's work both lacks and consciously relegates to the ethnographic sidelines. When he concludes his discussion of the near successful attempt of black radicals in Detroit to achieve municipal control he observes:

> Most ironic...is the very success of their failure: the representation - the model of this complex spatial dialectic - triumphantly survives in the form of a film and a book, but in the process of becoming an image and a spectacle, the referent seems to have disappeared, as so many people from Debord to Baudrillard always warned us it would (*ibid.*, p.415).

Two things emerge from this. Firstly, paradoxically, Jameson manages to speak about black struggles in Detroit without any qualms over being able to communicate his point. Secondly, any readership entering a dialogue with the film or book is a situated readership. That is, it brings its own context to the reading. Hence, making sense of the discourses of black radicalism is not stymied by abstract ideological meanings (closure) but opened up by the kind of dialogue readers generate with texts, discourses.

Interestingly, and contradictorily, Jameson goes on to suggest that what is referred to, that is, referents, have an impact on discourse. He notes:

> successful spatial representation...may be...inscribed in a narrative of defeat, which sometimes, even more effectively [than 'revolutionary triumph'], causes the whole architectonic of postmodern global space to rise up in

ghostly profile behind itself, as some ultimate dialectical barrier or invisible limit (*loc. cit.*).

To pursue the phenomenological analysis, Jameson has, in effect, extracted the sedimented event and comprehended it through its articulation (as film or book) with the historical present-as-postmodernity/globalisation of capital. Further, its very spectacular or mythical representation seems to provide the redemptive image, against the grain of commodification, through which the event can be recuperated. It is just this kind of representation (of an 'impossibility') which in Benjamin's terms places an event outside the historical process and thereby acts as a means through which the connection between the historical present and past can be understood.

It has been argued that Jameson's neglect of the everyday leads him to describe authentic or existential experience as in no way enabling us to grasp the complexities of global capitalism. On the contrary, Osborne (1995, pp.141-2) has argued, the narrativity of contemporary life cannot be understood without the kinds of process described above where the sedimented images of past presents are capable of interrupting the way the present is understood and reconnecting it to historical narrative.

As with Althusser, the weakness of Jameson is to neglect the situatedness of the commentator; the belief that totalisation can only be comprehended from an Olympian position rather than that of the situated subject. This point is confirmed by Jameson's emphasis on the Althusserian break between ideology and science which notoriously de-situates the knowing subject.

It also runs contrary to Jameson's more sensuous characterisations of cultural understanding through architecture - his description of the Gehry house (*ibid.*, pp.108-29), for example. The melange of motifs in postmodern architecture could be taken as an expression of the way the cultural dominant situates itself in relation to past presents and their motifs. The building itself becomes a referent here (*ibid.*, p.119) and serves to exemplify the kind of argument advanced in this discussion of Jameson, that is, that the building is self-referential, it both denotes itself as the architectural statement and expresses a relation to local geography and architectural tradition and its sedimented discursive senses. This dialectic is in fact read by Jameson as its own sense or *real* meaning.

Further, whilst the Gehry house carries connotations of past styles and usages, such as the play on the historically situated public-private spaces of buildings, Gehry house is predominantly shaped by the connotations of global socio-economic change which wrench the building away from its very subsidiary local symbolic charges. This is seen through the way the building subverts traditional notions of space and its usage, through for example, its 'tumbling cube' feature and use of facades which create a sense of uncertainty about the dimensions. (It is not possible to grasp the building via a photographic image.) Jameson concludes that the building primarily connotes highly abstract global forces and their spatial relations.

Now the strange thing about this account of the Gehry house is that the more familiar spatial aspects, the facades and connotations of earlier religious buildings, for example, are not seen as mediating the more abstract, global message, which, as it were, comes at us from out of the blue, although, of course, in Jameson's description itself, this is precisely what they do.

In other words, Jameson's description of the Gehry house actually suggests that far from being unmediated, its evocation of spatial complexity or abstractness is framed by the background of familiar features which suggest spatial abstraction through their arrangement in an unfamiliar (postmodern) configuration. This also suggests that the trope of abstractness here does not indicate something irretrievably beyond adequate description, but rather is only *relative to the familiar*, that which we take for granted.

In sum, Jameson's methodology rejects the duality of reference between the familiar, indexical features of statements and their articulation in the statement as the denotation of an object, in this case the relations of global capital. The indexical, everyday references are made and then dismissed, or in Jameson's (*op. cit.*, p.119) term 'volatilized', leaving the building as an impenetrable signifier which nonetheless expresses a material thought.

One of the least satisfactory aspects of Jameson's account of postmodern experience is his description of the retro or nostalgia mode. As Jameson notes, this is not the nostalgia of past associations but the wholesale recycling of the past as a series of motifs, graphics, styles of film acting, sepia-tinted images, art-deco, etc. However, he goes on to suggest (*ibid.*, xvii) that the forms of this 'nostalgia' can be separated from their (historical) content so that no questions are raised here about a real historical content to this experience. The idea of separating style from content raises the same difficulties as separating thoughts from their conceptual organisation, and would seem, remembering Frege's point about the impossibility of a world in which subjects (conceptual frameworks) are separated from their actual appearances, their usages in the world.

This in turn brings us to Osborne's (*op. cit.*, pp.194-6) discussion of Lefebvre's work on temporal objectification and the everyday. Jameson's description of the nostalgia mode corresponds to the objectification of temporalities which Lefebvre identifies with the commodification of time. In architecture, Jameson highlights '"historicism"...the random cannibalization of all the styles of the past...and, in general, what Henri Lefebvre has called the increasing primacy of the "neo"' (*ibid.*, p.18). Elsewhere, nostalgia is represented by 'historicist films...a depersonalised visual curiosity and a "return of the repressed" of the twenties and thirties "without affect"' (*ibid.*, xvii). Now whilst this counterposes the awakening to connotations of the past to a profound sense of distantiation, it could be suggested that the 'return of the repressed' is real enough and that the articulation or connotation of the historical present with the 'sutured' past can surely be found in the conditions of urban and economic life, the restructuring of capital, the resurgence of market hegemony and inequality which mirrors the 'twenties and 'thirties. A curious omission here is Thatcherism or Reagonomics which 'hark back' or articulate recent concerns with classical market liberalism. It is not clear why events noted in film studies, or more generally, 'art language' (*ibid.*, p.19) qualify as 'nostalgia' whilst those in political economy do not. Jameson seems to have fallen victim to his own critique; as Osborne (1994, p.3) indicates, for Fukuyama, and Jameson, the past is past but the present knows no limits.

The Politics of Time

Feuerbach's insistence on the continuing access to the past in its simultaneity with the present was aimed at Hegel's closure of the past via *Aufhebung*. Jameson's perennial engagement with the place of the historical past in *Postmodernism* in some ways rehearses that debate. However, whereas for Feuerbach, life could correct abstract thought, ideology, in Jameson, abstract ideological signifiers effect historical closure. There is a pervasive pessimism that the everyday has lost touch with the (now) global realities and cannot dislodge the ideological signifier.

Against this, as Osborne (*op. cit.*, p.196) argues, Lefebvre's two-fold dynamic sees the cycles of capitalism's restructuring and renovation both producing commodified time and as being undermined by the structures through which these repetitions are received. The open horizon or continuous present of the everyday both reconnects, articulates the historical past with the present and in doing so the repetition punctuates the everyday with a sense of the genuinely novel character of the historical present.

Whilst one aspect of the everyday, its very indexicality, connotes the past, on the other side it indexes the genuinely new features of the cultural dominant. In other words, 'today' it picks out its enormous and spontaneous historical reflexivity, its access to the past in the recycling of past styles and its reassembly of these in historicist or other discursive forms - as Jameson's account of postmodernism uniquely indicates.

Finally, Osborne (1995, pp.192-3) argues that Lefebvre's account of the everyday offers a new basis for an emancipatory project, in that whilst the notion of alienation in the early Marx was criticised as anthropologism, the new position locates emancipatory critique in the structures of the world itself. Hence a politics of time is exigent, a contestation of the cultural tropes of closure is required which persuades people of 'The simple possibility that things might proceed otherwise' (Osborne, 1994, p.3).

Notes

[1]   See discussion of Mandel (1978) in Jameson (1991, xx).

[2]   It is important to distinguish between denotation in Barthes and Dummett, as for the latter denotation is facilitated by context rather than conventional usage itself. In terms of linguistic closure Dummett therefore has radically different implications.

[3]   The complexity seems to require reference to a globalised space which decentres its objects - but is this so very different from orthodox structuralist ideas when applied to globalisation?

[4]   Harvey Milk was a gay rights activist in San Francisco.

[5]   A 'name' in Frege-Dummett refers to a phrase, expression or term which picks out an object/topic in context. Whether this is described as referent or reference is arguably of secondary importance to the reality of the sense linked to the object. Referent and reference arguably merge at the point where a speaker grasps the sense of a situation. Therefore physicality, or embodiment, following the argument of Chapter 6, could be seen as having an ideational aspect where the objects of discursive practices always appear as inscribed or sedimented within fields of reference.

[6]   The indexical, taken for granted nature of context entails that self-evidence (making sense) does not work like logical relations where formal definitions are employed (Dummett, *op. cit.*, p.336) and therefore does not require synonymy between elements of utterances. Articulation is therefore non-reductionist either to elements or whole/meaning convention in contrast to the fixed meaning conventions of semiotics or Foucault's prioritisation of discursive elements (Laclau and Mouffe, 1989, p.107).

[7]   'Original meaning' is here understood as 'past-present' comprehension (see Note 8).

[8]   Sedimentation is taken as occurring in cycles where historical presents become past presents. Such presents are typified by a specific cultural horizon of expectations which circumscribes what is deemed practicable and desirable within the present times or temporality (Heller, 1982, pp.44). Hence sedimentation refers to what is recoupable from that cycle (past present) as a 'present-past'.

8   Afterword

The different rhythms experienced in the temporalisation of routine are well enough illustrated in Jameson's account of downtown life in contemporary Los Angeles. It is then arguable that Jameson's account of late capitalism, despite his claims to the contrary, tells us in essence what we need to know about global market forces. His own suggestion that this postmodern experience is an unrepresentable state of affairs, may owe as much to the semiotics of representation as to any substantive problem. It may just be that the elusive topic emerges from a reading of *Postmodernism* which, ironically, *contextualises* the 'effacement of history', as a visible articulation of this new temporalisation.

At least we can see from the text that the contemporaneity it describes consists in a complex conjuncture of rhythmic structures of different temporalities or locales in a new articulation under a cultural dominance of an increasingly globalised capital. Globalisation itself gives these developments a new everyday tempo such that place is destabilised towards space and the consequent hybridisation of place and identity tends to undermine the logics of the nation state and the absolutisation of 'the other', though the interaction with a deabsolutised Other is no guarantee of a harmonious intersubjectivity, as recent events in the Balkans have testified. On the other hand, we know from Merleau-Ponty's *ambiguitié* and Hegel's 'master-slave dialectic' that the lord only comes to know himself through the bondsman's activity and that this contradictory intersubjectivity is also a source of knowledge and power, the *sens* of the subject through which emancipation is possible.[1]

For Merleau-Ponty, the underlying forms of social organisation, of institution and situation, remain open as different articulations of the cultural dominant and its temporal structure. Now Weberians and discourse theorists have defined the locus of organisation as 'out there', whether in terms of the operations of the language of discourse or of specific institutional factors of bureaucratisation. The work of Schutz, Merleau-Ponty and Dummett has, at least by implication, opposed this overconventionalised view of social reality as a closed system of classification and objectification.

Schutz's important achievement, a radical reading of the

rationalisation thesis, places the latter within an 'open horizon of typical familiarity', the routine, everyday structure of experience, where hypostatised goals are always open to alternative interpretations, to contestation and reclamation of these fetishised institutional forms.

Dummett's reading of Frege's theory of meaning enables us to locate the routine, contextualised nature of our discursive practices in terms of their senses, which connect the conventionalised, sedimented meanings of utterances to their present deployment, thus realising their existential meaning and reference. The articulation of conventionalised language with the present context renders visible its sedimented content in such a way as to transfigure its meaning and thereby release a new reference. Here, the meaning routines of one type of context (of past utterances) find themselves in conjunction with those of another. This interruption of routine as an assimilation to a present context (pattern of routines) has a quality of surprise or revelation (despite Heidegger's perception of it as merely 'diversification').

This de-fetishisation of language and release of a new content is perhaps most recently illustrated in the interruption of the onward march of neo- and social Darwinist discourses through the debates around GM foods. The progression of these teleologies of evolutionary closure would have seemed all but inexorable in the recent past, but in 1999, the debates about the context of genetically modified foods have opened up the field of related issues. This has revealed the links between science and global capital and thus challenged the objectivist stance of scientific practitioners.[2] The everyday basis of scientific discoveries is shown as imbricated within the routines of transnational corporations. Hence we can see scientific rationalisation as containing the marks of its context of enunciation. As Garfinkel (*op. cit.*, pp.3-4) notes, the

> impersonality, or objectivity of accounts [is] not independent of the socially organised occasions of their use. Members' accounts...are *features* of the socially organised occasions of their use.

Here a crisis of science, the moment of referencing the context, its actual topic, against its objectivist claims, demonstrates the radical epiphanic power of the everyday.

Notes

1. See Kruks (1990, p.121) and Silverman (1987, p.82ff) on the significance of ambiguity in Merleau-Ponty's work on intersubjectivity; see Hegel (1966) on 'Lordship and Bondage', on the ambiguous nature of domination over a determinate subject.

2. See Vidal (1999) for example, on Indian peasants' struggles against dependency on global capital via campaigns against self-destructing crops ('terminator seeds') which is part of a more generalised creeping dependency for crop propagation.

Bibliography

Adorno, T. (1973), *Negative Dialectics*, (trans. E.B. Ashton), Routledge & Kegan Paul, London.

Adorno, T. (ed. J. Bernstein) (1991), *The Culture Industry: Selected Essays on Mass Culture*, Routledge, London.

Adorno, T. and Horkheimer, M. (1989), *Dialectic of Enlightenment*, Verso, London.

Althusser, L. (1971), 'Ideology and Ideological State Apparatuses' in L. Althusser (ed.), *Lenin and Philosophy and Other Essays*, New Left Books, London.

Althusser, L. (1977), *For Marx*, New Left Books, London.

Althusser, L and Balibar, E. (1975), *Reading Capital*, New Left Books, London.

Austin, J.L. (1961), 'A Plea for Excuses', in J.O. Urmson and G.J. Warnock (eds.), *Philosophical Papers*, Oxford University Press, Oxford.

Austin, J.L. (1980), *How to do Things with Words*, J. Urmson and M. Sbisa (eds.), Oxford University Press, Oxford.

Barnes, B. (1974), *Scientific Knowledge and Social Theory*, Routledge & Kegan Paul, London.

Barthes, R. (1972), *Mythologies*, Cape, London.

Barthes, R. (1975), *The Pleasure of the Text*, Hall and Wang, New York.

Baudrillard, J. (1988), *Selected Writings*, Polity Press, Cambridge.

Bauman, Z. (1991), *Modernity and the Holocaust*, Polity Press in association with Blackwell Publishers, Oxford.

Beardsley, M.C. (1958), *Aesthetics*, Harcourt Brace and World, New York.

Benjamin, J. (1990), *The Bonds of Love: Psychoanalysis, Feminism and the Problem of Domination*, Virago Press, London.

Benjamin, W. (1985), 'Central Park', *New German Critique*, vol. 34.

Benson, D. and Hughes, J. (1983), *The Perspective of Ethnomethodology*, Longman, London and New York.

Benton, T. (1984), *The Rise and Fall of Structural Marxism: Althusser and his Influence*, Macmillan, London.

Benveniste, E. (1971), *Problems in General Linguistics*, (trans. M.E. Meek), University of Miami Press, Florida.

Butler, J. (1996), 'Gender as Performance', in P. Osborne, (ed.), *A Critical Sense: Interviews with Intellectuals*, Routledge, London, pp. 109-126.

Callinicos, A. (1982), *Is There a Future for Marxism?*, Macmillan, London.

Carl, W. (1994), *Frege's Theory of Sense and Reference: its Origins and Scope*, Cambridge University Press, Cambridge.

Collier, A. (1991), 'The Ethics in the "Ethics"', *Studia Spinozana*, vol. 7, pp. 69-93.

Collingwood, R.G. (1994), *The Idea of History*, Oxford University Press, Oxford and New York.

Cousins, H.M. and Hussain, A. (1984), *Michel Foucault*, Macmillan London.

Couturat, L. (1901), *La Logique de Leibniz d'après des Documents inédits*, Alcan, Paris.

D'Amico, R. (1989), *Historicism and Knowledge*, Routledge, London.

Davidson, D. (1977), 'The Method of Truth in Metaphysics', in P.A. French, T.E. Uehling, Jr., and H.K. Wettstein (eds.), *Studies in the Philosophy of Language*, Morris, Minnesota, pp.244-254.

Davidson, D. (1979), 'What Metaphors Mean', in S. Sacks (ed.), *On Metaphor*, University of Chicago Press, Chicago.

Davidson, D. (1984), *Inquiries into Truth and Interpretation*, Clarendon Press, Oxford.

Davidson, D. (1986), 'A Coherence Theory of Truth and Knowledge', in E. Lepore (ed.) *Truth and Interpretation*, Blackwell, Oxford.

Debord, G. (1981), 'Perspectives for Conscious Alterations in Everyday Life', *The Situationist International Anthology*, (ed. K. Knabb), Bureau of Public Secrets, Berkeley.

Denzin, N.K. (1992), *Symbolic Interactionism and Cultural Studies: The Politics of Interpretation*, Blackwell, Oxford.

Derrida, J. (trans. F.C.T. Moore) (1974), 'White Mythology', in *New Literary History*, 6, vol. 1, pp. 5-74.

Dews, P. (1986), 'Adorno, Poststructuralism and the Critique of Identity', *New Left Review*, vol. 157, pp. 28-44.

Donald, J. and Hall, S. (eds.) (1986), *Politics and Ideology*, Open University Press, Milton Keynes.

Drabble, M. (1977), *The Ice Age*, Weidenfeld and Nicolson, London.

Dummett, M. (1981), *The Interpretation of Frege's Philosophy*, Harvard University Press, Cambridge, Mass.

Durkheim, E. (1982), *The Rules of Sociological Method*, Macmillan, London.

Elliott, G. (1998), 'Ghostlier Demarcations: on the Posthumous Edition of Althusser's Writings', *Radical Philosophy*, vol. 90, pp. 20-32.

Empson, W. (1985), *The Structure of Complex Words*, The Hogarth Press, London.

Farrell, F.B. (1994), *Subjectivity, Realism and Postmodernism: the Recovery of the World in Recent Philosophy*, Cambridge University Press, Cambridge.

Feuerbach, L. (1983), 'Towards a Critique of Hegelian Philosophy', in L.S. Steppelvitch (ed. and intro.), *The Young Hegelians*, Cambridge University Press, Cambridge.

Feuerbach, L. (1986), *Principles of the Philosophy of the Future*, Hackett, Indianapolis.

Foucault, M. (1971), 'Orders of Discourse', *Social Science Information*, 10, vol. 2, pp. 7-30.

Foucault, M. (1977a), *Discipline and Punish*, London, Tavistock.

Foucault, M. (1977b), 'Nietzsche, Genealogy, History', *Language, Counter-Memory, Practice*, Blackwell, Oxford.

Foucault, M. (1979), *The History of Sexuality, Vol. 1*, Allen Lane, London.

Foucault, M. (1980) *Power/Knowledge: Selected Interviews and Other Writings 1972-77*, Harvester Press, Hassocks, Sussex.

Fraser, N. (1989), 'Solidarity or Singularity? Richard Rorty between Romanticism and Technocracy' in N. Fraser (ed.), *Unruly Practices: Power, Discourse and Gender in Contemporary Social Theory*, University of Minnesota Press, Minneapolis.

Frege, G. (1952), 'On Sense and Reference', in M. Black and P. Geach (trans.), *Philosophical Writings of Gottlob Frege*, Blackwell, Oxford.

Frege, G, (1964) *The Basic Laws of Arithmetic (Grundlagen)*, (trans. and ed. M. Furth), Berkeley and Los Angeles.

Friedan, B. (1972), *The Feminine Mystique*, Penguin, Harmondsworth.

Fukuyama, F. (1992), *The End of History and the Last Man*, Penguin, Harmondsworth.

Gadamer, H-G. (1977), 'On the Scope and Function of Hermeneutical Reflection' in H-G. Gadamer, (ed. and trans. D. Linge), *Philosophical Reflections*, University of California Press, Berkeley.

Gadamer, H-G. (1981), *Truth and Method*, Sheed and Ward. London.

Garfinkel, H. (1967), *Studies in Ethnomethodology*, Prentice Hall, Englewood Cliffs.

Gay, du, P. (1997), 'Organizing Identity: Making Up People at Work' in Du Gay (ed.) (1997), *op. cit.*

Gay, du, P. (ed.) (1997), *Production of Culture/Cultures of Production*, Culture, Media and Identities Series, Course Chair, S. Hall, Sage in association with The Open University.

Gay, du, P. , *et al.* (1997), *Doing Cultural Studies: The Story of the Sony Walkman*, Culture, Media and Identities Series, Course Chair, S. Hall, Sage in association with The Open University.

Giddens, A. (1979), *Central Problems in Social Theory: Action. Structure and Contradiction in Social Analysis*, Macmillan, London and Basingstoke.

Giddens, A. (1984), *The Constitution of Society*, Polity Press, Cambridge.

Giddens, A. (1990), *The Consequences of Modernity*, Polity Press, Cambridge.

Giddens, A. (1991), *Modernity and Self-identity: Self and Society in the Late Modern Age*, Polity Press, Cambridge.

Giddens, A. (1994), *Beyond Left and Right*, Polity Press, Cambridge.

Godelier, M. (1986), *The Mental and the Material: Thought, Economy and Society*, Verso, London.

Goffman, E. (1968), *Asylums*, Penguin, Harmondsworth.

Goffman, E. (1982), *The Presentation of Self in Everyday Life*, Penguin, Harmondsworth.

Gramsci, A. (1971), (ed. and trans. Q. Hoare and G. Nowell Smith), *Selections from the Prison Notebooks*, Lawrence and Wishart, London.

Grayling, A.C. (1985), *The Refutation of Scepticism*, Open Court Publishing, La Salle.

Greimas, A.J. (1983), *Structural Semantics: an Attempt at a Method*, (trans. D. McDowell, R. Schleifer and A. Velie), University of Nebraska Press, Lincoln.

Grimshaw, J. (1996), 'Philosophy, Feminism and Universalism', *Radical Philosophy*, vol. 76, pp. 19-28.

Habermas, J. (1970), 'Knowledge and Interest', in D. Emmet and A. MacIntyre (eds.), *Sociological Theory and Philosophical Analysis*, Macmillan, London and Basingstoke, 36-54.

Habermas, J. (1977), 'A Review of Gadamer's Truth and Method', in F. Dallmayr and T. McCarthy (eds.), *Understanding and Social Enquiry*, Notre Dame University Press, Notre Dame.

Habermas, J. (1980), 'The Hermeneutic Claim to Universality', in J. Bleicher (ed.), *Contemporary Hermeneutics: Method, Philosophy and Critique*, Routledge and Kegan Paul, London.

Habermas, J. (1987a), *The Theory of Communicative Action, vol. 1*, (trans. T. McCarthy), Polity Press, Cambridge.

Habermas, J. (1987b) *The Theory of Communicative Action, vol. 2*, (trans. T. McCarthy), Polity Press, Cambridge.

Habermas, J. (1991), *The Philosophical Discourse of Modernity*, Polity Press, Cambridge.

Hacking, I. (1976), 'Individual Substance', in H.G. Frankfurt (ed.), *Leibniz: a Collection of Critical Essays*, University of Notre Dame Press, Notre Dame and London, pp. 137-154.

Hall, S. (1986), 'Politics and Ideology: a Contemporary Case', Cassette 2, Side 1, *Course DE 354, Beliefs and Ideologies*, Open University Press, Milton Keynes.

Hall, S. (1986), 'Variants of Liberalism' in J. Donald and S. Hall (eds.) (1986), *op. cit.*

Hall, S. (1990), 'Cultural Identity and Diaspora', in J. Rutherford (ed.), *Identity: Community, Culture, Difference*, Lawrence and Wishart, London.

Hall, S. (1997), 'The Work of Representation', in S. Hall (ed.) (1997), *op. cit.*

Hall, S. (ed.) (1997), *Representation*, Sage Publications in association with the Open University, London.

Hall, S. (ed.) (1997), *Representation: Cultural Representations and Signifying Practices*, Culture, Media and Identity Series, Course Chair, S. Hall, Sage in association with The Open University.

Hegel, G.W.F. (1966), *The Phenomenology of Mind*, (trans. and introduction J. Baillie), George Allen & Unwin, London.

Heidegger, M. (1962), *Being and Time*, (Trans. J. McQuarrie and E. Robinson), Blackwell, Oxford.

Heller, A. (1982), *A Theory of History*, Routledge & Kegan Paul, London.

Heller, A, (1984), *Everyday Life*, Routledge & Kegan Paul, London.

Hines, B. (1981), *Looks and Smiles*, Michael Joseph, London.

Hull, C.L. (1997), 'The Need in Thinking: Materiality in Theodor, W. Adorno and Judith Butler', in *Radical Philosophy*, vol. 84, pp.22-35.

Husserl, E. (trans. D. Cairns) (1960), *Cartesian Meditations*, Nijhoff, The Hague.

Husserl, E. (1970), 'The Origin of Geometry', in E. Husserl (ed. and trans. D. Carr) (1970), *op. cit.*, pp. 353-78.

Husserl, E. (ed. and trans. D. Carr) (1970), *The Crisis of the European Sciences and Transcendental Phenomenology*, Northwestern University Press, Evanston.

Jakobson, R. (1971), 'Results of the Conference of Anthropologists and Linguists', *Selected Writings, vol. 2, Word and Language*, Mouton, Paris and The Hague.

Jameson, F. (1984), 'Postmodernism, or the Cultural Logic of Late Capitalism', *New Left Review*, vol. 146, pp. 53-92.

Jameson, F. (1991), *Postmodernism or the Cultural Logic of Late Capitalism*, Verso, London.

Keane, J. (1988), 'More Theses on the Philosophy of History', in Skinner, *op. cit.*

Keat, R. and Urry, J. (1975), *Social Theory as Science*, Routledge, London and Boston.

Komesaroff, P. (1986), *Objectivity, Science and Society: Interpreting Nature and Society in the Age of the Crisis of Science*, Routledge & Kegan Paul, London.

Kraniauskas, J. (1998), 'Globalisation is Ordinary: The Transnationalisation of Cultural Studies', *Radical Philosophy*, Vol. 90, pp. 9-19.

Kripke, S. (1979), *Naming and Necessity*, Oxford.

Kruks, S. (1990), *Situation and Human Existence: Freedom, Subjectivity and Society*, Unwin Hyman, London.

Kuhn, T.S. (1970), *The Structure of Scientific Revolutions*, University of Chicago Press, London.

Lacan, J. (1977), *Ecrits: A Selection*, Tavistock, London.

Laclau, E. (1987), *Politics and Ideology in Marxist Theory*, New Left Books, London.

Laclau, E. and Mouffe, C. (1989), *Hegemony and Socialist Strategy*, Verso, London.

Laclau, E. and Mouffe, C. (1990), 'PostMarxism Without Apologies', in E. Laclau (ed.), *New Reflections on the Revolution of our Time*, Verso, London.

Lakatos, I. (1970), Falsification and the Methodology of Scientific Research Programmes', in I. Lakatos and A. Musgrave (eds.), *Criticism and the Growth of Knowledge*, Cambridge University Press, London.

Laplanche, J. and Pontalis, J.B. (1967), *Vocabulaire de la Psychoanalyse*, Paris.

Le Doeuff, M. (1991), *Hipparchia's Choice*, (trans. T. Selous), Blackwell, Oxford.

Lefebvre, H. (1971), *Everyday Life in the Modern World*, (trans. S. Rabinovitch), Allen Lane, London.

Lefebvre, H. (1987), 'The Everyday and Everydayness', in A. Kaplan and K. Ross (eds.) *Yale French Studies*, vol. 73, special issue on 'Everyday Life'.

150 *Intersubjectivity and Contemporary Social Theory*

Lefebvre, H. (1991), *Critique of Everyday Life, Volume 1*, 'Introduction', (trans. J. Moore), Verso, London and New York.
Levi-Strauss, C. (1964), *Totemism*, Merlin Press, London.
Locke, J. (1966), 'Second Treatise on Civil Government: An Essay Concerning the True Original, Extent and End of Civil Government', in E. Barker (intro.), *Social Contract: Essays by Locke, Hume and Rousseau*, Oxford University Press, London.
Lockwood, D. (1981), 'The Weakest Link in the Chain? Some Comments on the Marxist Theory of Action', in R.L. and H.I. Simpson (eds.), *Research in the Sociology of Work*, vol. 1, pp. 435-81.
Lyotard, J-F. (1984), *The Postmodern Condition. A Report on Knowledge*, Manchester University Press, Manchester.
MacIntyre, A. (1985), 'Relativism, Power and Philosophy', *Proceedings and Addresses of the American Philosophical Association*, A.P.A., Newark, Delaware.
MacKay, H. (ed.) (1997), *Consumption and Everyday Life*, Culture, Media and Identity Series, Course Chair, S. Hall, Sage in association with The Open University.
Mandel, E. (1978), *Late Capitalism*, NLB, London.
Mannheim, K. (1969), 'Limits of the Sociological Approach to Personality and the Emergence of the New Democratic Idea of Planning', in K. Mannheim (ed.), *Essays on Sociology and Social Psychology*, Routledge & Kegan Paul, London.
Marx, K. (1970), *Economic and Philosophic Manuscripts of 1844*, (ed. and intro. D. Struik), Lawrence and Wishart, London.
Marx, K. (1974), *Capital, Vol. 1*, Lawrence and Wishart, London.
McDowell, J. (1977), 'On the Sense and Reference of a Proper Name', in *Mind*, vol. LXXXVI, pp.159-185.
McDowell, J. (1994), *Mind and World*, Harvard University Press, London.
McNay, L. (1994), *Foucault: a Critical Introduction*, Continuum, New York.
Mead, G.H. (1970), *Mind, Self and Society*, University of Chicago Press, London.
Merleau-Ponty, M. (1971), *Humanism and Terror: An Essay on the Communist Problem*, (trans. with notes, J. O'Neill), Beacon Press, Boston.
Merleau-Ponty, M. (1971), *Sense and Non-Sense*, (trans. H.L. and P.A. Dreyfus), Northwestern University Press, Evanston.
Merleau-Ponty, M. (1992), (trans. C. Smith), *Phenomenology of Perception*, Routledge, London.
Monk, R. (1996), *Bertrand Russell: the Spirit of Solitude*, Jonathan Cape, London.
Moores, S. (1997), 'Broadcasting and its Audiences', in J. Mackay (ed.) (*op. cit.*), pp. 213-58.
Mouffe, C. (1981), 'Hegemony and Ideology in Gramsci', in T. Bennett *et al.* (eds.), *Culture, Ideology and Social Process*, Batsford in association with the Open University Press, London.
Negus, K. (1997), 'The Production of Culture', in du Gay (ed.) *op. cit.*, pp. 67-118.

Nisbet, R.A. (1972), *The Sociological Tradition*, Heineman, London.

O'Neill, J. (1995), *The Poverty of Postmodernism*, Routledge, London and New York.

Osborne, P. (1992), 'Modernity is a Qualitative, not a Quantitative Category', *New Left Review*, vol. 192, pp. 65-84.

Osborne, P. (1994), 'The Politics of Time', *Radical Philosophy*, vol. 68, pp. 3-9.

Osborne, P. (1995), *The Politics of Time: Modernity and the Avant-Garde*, Verso, London and New York.

Pivcevic, E. (1986), *The Concept of Reality*, Duckworth, London.

Popper, K. (1968), *The Logic of Scientific Discovery*, Routledge & Kegan Paul, London.

Popper, K. (1972), *Objective Knowledge*, Clarendon Press, Oxford.

Quine, W.V.O. (1969), *Ontological Relativity and Other Essays*, Columbia University Press, New York.

Ricoeur, P. (1986), *The Rule of Metaphor*, Routledge, London.

Rorty, R. (1979), *Philosophy and the Mirror of Nature*, University Press, Princeton, N.J.

Rorty, R. (1982), 'Pragmatism, Relativism and Irrationalism', in R. Rorty (ed.), *Consequences of Pragmatism*, University of Minnesota Press, Minneapolis.

Rorty, R. (1986), 'Pragamatism, Davidson and Truth', in E. le Pore (ed.), *Truth and Interpretation*, Blackwell, Oxford.

Rorty, R. (1989), *Contingency, Irony and Solidarity*, Cambridge University Press, Cambridge.

Rorty, R. (1991), *Objectivity, Relativism and Truth*, Cambridge University Press, Cambridge.

Rorty, R. (1991a), 'Feminism and Pragmatism', *Radical Philosophy*, vol. 59, pp. 3-14.

Rorty, R. (1993), 'Feminism, Ideology and Deconstruction: A Pragmatist View', *Hypatia 8*, vol. 2, pp. 96-103.

Rosa, H. (1996), 'Goods and Life-Forms; Relativism in Charles Taylor's Political Philosophy', *Radical Philosophy*, vol. 71, pp. 20-26.

Rose, G. (1995), *Hegel Contra Sociology*, Athlone Press, London.

Russell, B. (1965a), *An Enquiry into Meaning and Truth*, Penguin, Harmondsworth.

Russell, B. (1965b), 'Mr. Strawson on Referring', in R.R. Ammerman (ed.), *Classics of Analytical Philosophy*, McGraw-Hill, New York.

Russell, B. (1973), 'On Denoting', in D. Lackey (ed.), *Bertrand Russell: Essays in Analysis*, George Allen & Unwin, London.

Saussure, de., F. (1974), *Course in General Linguistics*, Fontana/Collins, London.

Schleifer, R. (1987), *A.J. Greimas and the Nature of Meaning: Linguistics, Semiotics and Discourse Theory*, Croom Helm, London and Sydney.

Schutz, A. (1967), *Collected Papers, vol. 1: The Problem of Social Reality* (ed. M. Natanson), Martinus Nijhoff, The Hague.

Schutz, A. (1970a), 'Concept and Theory Formation in the Social Sciences', in D. Emmet and A. MacIntyre (eds.), *Sociological Theory and Philosophical Analysis*, Macmillan, London and Basingstoke, pp. 1-19, also in Schutz, A. (1967), vol. 1.

Schutz, A. (1970b), 'The Problem of Rationality in the Social World', *op. cit.*, pp. 89-114, also in Schutz (1967), vol. 2.

Schwarz, B. (1986), 'Conservatism, Nationalism, Imperialism', in J. Donald and S. Hall (eds.), *Politics and Ideology*, Open University Press, Milton Keynes.

Shilling, C. (1997), 'The Body and Difference' in K. Woodward (ed.), *Identity and Difference*, Sage Publications in association with the Open University.

Silverman, D. and Torode, B. (1980), *The Material Word: Some Theories of Language and its Limits*, Routledge & Kegan Paul, London.

Silverman, H.J. (1987), *Inscriptions Between Structuralism and Phenomenology*, Routledge, London.

Simmel, G. (1971), 'The Metropolis and Mental Life', in K. Thompson and J. Tunstall (eds.), *Sociological Perspectives*, Penguin Books in association with The Open University Press, Harmondsworth.

Skinner, Q. (1988), *Meaning and Context: Quentin Skinner and his Critics*, J. Tully (ed.), Polity Press, Cambridge.

Smart, B. (1976), *Sociology, Phenomenology and Marxian Analysis; a Critical Discussion of the Theory and Practice of a Science of Society*, Routledge & Kegan Paul, London.

Spinoza, B. (intro. T.S. Gregory and trans. A. Boyle) (1986), *Spinoza's Ethics and on the Correction of the Understanding*, Dent, London.

Strauss, A. (1964), *Psychiatric Institutions and Ideologies*, Free Press.

Taylor, C. (1988), 'The Hermeneutics Conflict', in Skinner, *op. cit.*

Thompson, K. (ed.) (1997), *Media and Cultural Regulation*, Culture, Media and Identity Series, Course Chair, S. Hall, Sage in association with The Open University.

Thrift, N. (1997), '"Us and Them": Re-imagining Places, Re-imagining Identities', in J. Mackay (ed.) (*op. cit.*), pp. 159-212.

Vidal, J. (1999), 'The Seeds of Wrath', in *The Guardian Weekend*, 19.6.99, pp. 10-19.

Volosinov, V.N. (1973), *Marxism and the Philosophy of Language*, Seminar Press, New York.

Wagner, H. (1973), 'The Scope of Phenomenological Sociology: Considerations and Suggestions', in G. Psathas (ed.), *Phenomenological Sociology*, Wiley, London.

Warnke, G. (1987), *Gadamer: Hermeneutics, Tradition and Reason*, Stanford University Press, Stanford, California.

Weber, M. (1976), *The Protestant Ethic and the Spirit of Capitalism*, Allen and Unwin, London.

Wellmer, A. (1985), *Zur Dialektik von Moderne und Postmoderne*, Frankfurt.

Wellmer, A. (1986), 'Zur Kritik der Diskursethic', in *Ethik und Dialog*, Frankfurt.

Whitehead, P. (1985), *The Writing on the Wall*, Michael Joseph, London.
Wilson, C. (1992), 'How did the Dinosaurs die out? How did the Poets Survive?', *Radical Philosophy*, vol. 62, p. 20.
Winch, P. (1970), *The Idea of a Social Science and its Relation to Philosophy*, Routledge & Kegan Paul, London.
Wittgenstein, L. (1989), Philosophical Investigations, Blackwell, Oxford.
Worsley, P. (1978), *Introducing Sociology*, Penguin Books, Harmondsworth.
Woodward, K. (ed.) (1997), *Identity and Difference*, Culture, Media and Identity Series, Course Chair, S. Hall, Sage in association with The Open University.
Wrong, D. (1961), 'The Oversocialised Conception of Man in Modern Sociology', *The American Sociological Review*, vol. xxvi, pp. 184-193.

Index

Abstract Objects
    literary topics 89
    problem of reference 89, 94
    rooted in the everyday 89
Adorno ix
    and constellation 24, 26
    identity thinking 61, 114-115
Althusser, L. 11, 132
    and realism 68
    'essential section' 133
    ideology and phenomenology 68-69
    interpellation 65
    overdetermination 64
    Spinozist reading of 66
    the category of the subject 67
Ambiguity
    between conventional and denotative
    reference 108
Aristotle 32, 41
    metaphor and actualisation 75
Articulation 49-52, 133
    and self-evidence 130-131, 139-140
    as making sense 130, 139
    Dummett on 130
    Hall on Gramsci and 129
    non-reductionist 139-140
Austin, J.L. 53-54, 114

Barnes, B. 52
Barthes, R.
    denotation and connotation 121-123
    denotation differs from Frege 124
    phenomenological critique 73
    semiotics 72-73
    reader of myths as unsituated 121
Base-superstructure perspective ix
    Althusser's rejection of 99, 107
    as generalised 99-100

Bauman, Z
    and the Holocaust 9
Beardsley, M.C.
    contradiction and metaphorical unity
    63
Benjamin, J. 7
Benjamin, W. 136
    historical dislocation 134
    redemption of the past 134
Benson, D. and Hughes, J. 111-112
Benton, T. 48
    Gramsci and rationality 48
Benveniste, E.
    limitation of polysemy 76-77
Bôcher, M.
    names as symbols not entities 80
Bureaucracy 8ff
Body, the
    and body language 116
    and social construction 102-105
    see also embodiment
Butler, J. 105-106
    performativity 102

Callinicos, A.
    separation of language and world 72
Collier, A. 67
    materiality of ideas 67, 90
Collingwood, R.G.
    and historical explanation 53
Common sense 21, 110
    See also Gramsci 48ff
    and Merleau-Ponty's *prejuge du*
    monde 105
    and open, sedimented, polysemic
    character 133
Communication
    and identification 57
    and semiotics 91-92